GODLESS MORALITY

Let God Arise (Mowbray) 1972

New Vision of Glory (Mowbray) 1974

A New Heaven (Mowbray) 1979

Beyond Belief (Mowbray) 1981

Signs of Glory (Darton, Longman & Todd) 1982

The Killing[1] (Darton, Longman & Todd)

The Anglican Tradition (ed.) (Mowbray) 1984

Paradoxes of Christian Faith and Life (Mowbray) 1984

The Sidelong Glance (Darton, Longman & Todd) 1985

The Way of the Cross[2] (Collins) 1986

Seven to Flee, Seven to Follow (Mowbray) 1986

Crossfire: Faith and Doubt in an Age of Certainty (Collins)
    1988

The Divine Risk (ed.) (Darton, Longman & Todd) 1990

Another Country, Another King (Collins) 1991

Who Needs Feminism (SPCK) 1991

Anger, Sex, Doubt and Death (SPCK) 1992

The Stranger in the Wings (SPCK) 1994

Churches and How to Survive Them – co-author, Brice
    Avery (HarperCollins) 1994

Behold Your King[3] (SPCK) 1995

Limping Towards the Sunrise (The St Andrew Press) 1996

Dancing on the Edge (HarperCollins) 1997

1. Winner of the Winifred Mary Stanford Award
2. The Archbishop of Canterbury's Lent Book (1986)
3. Revised and expanded version of *The Killing* (1984)

GODLESS MORALITY

Keeping Religion out of Ethics

Richard Holloway

CANONGATE

First published in Great Britain in 1999
by Canongate Books Ltd, 14 High Street, Edinburgh EH1 1TE

10 9 8 7 6 5 4 3 2

British Library Cataloguing-in-Publication Data
A catalogue record for this book is available on
request from the British Library

ISBN 0 86241 909 3

Typeset by Hewer Text Ltd, Edinburgh
Printed and bound by Biddles Ltd, Guildford and Kings Lynn

For Jim and Pat

Contents

Preface

I would like to thank Gresham College in the City of London for giving me the opportunity to think about the themes that are expanded in this book. I would also like to express my gratitude to the Human Fertilisation and Embryology Authority, of which I was a member for its first seven years. During that time I was exposed to the complex and problematic world of reproductive technology and the science and ethics that underlie it. With few exceptions, I was impressed by the integrity of the scientists and clinicians I met, as well as by the quality of the other members of the HFEA. Those years on the HFEA forced me to confront many of the issues that are explored in this book.

As always, I am particularly grateful to my secretary, Christine Roy, not only for helping me with this book, but for her assistance in handling the complexities of a busy life. Jamie Byng of Canongate has been a great encourager in the writing of this book and I am most grateful to him.

Richard Holloway
April 1999

Acknowledgements

There are several extracts from other publications in this book, and we are grateful to the following publishers for their permission to use them. For the passages from Genesis (NRSV), the Division of Christian Education of the National Council of the Churches of Christ in the United States of America; for 'Senex' from John Betjeman's *Church Poems*, John Murray (Publishers) Ltd; for 'Epitaph on an Army of Mercenaries' by A.E. Housman, The Society of Authors as the literary representatives of A.E. Housman. The passage from *The Proper Study of Mankind* by Isaiah Berlin is reproduced with permission of Curtis Brown Ltd, London on behalf of The Isaiah Berlin Literary Trust Copyright © Isaiah Berlin 1958, 1969.

Introduction

Do we have to be religious to be moral? Do we have to believe in God to be good? These questions may sound impertinent to people without a religion or clear belief in God who are trying to lead a good life. In fact, unbelievers could easily react to these questions with ironic laughter as they think of all the crimes committed in the name of religion, the wars fought on behalf of religion, and the guilt and misery that has been imposed upon human beings who have deviated from religious norms in societies where religion has been in a position of authority. This failure to connect the lamentable record of religion with the high claims that religious leaders make and the exhortations they issue is bad enough; what is almost as intolerable is the patronising attitude they sometimes adopt towards highly moral people who have no religion and feel no need to have one. Many religious leaders say that without a belief in God and in absolute standards there can be no genuine moral conduct; that the moral confusions of our own time are directly related to the erosion of religion in Western society.

It is true that most religions have particular moral codes and, even if they are more often honoured in the breach than in the observance, they can help to create a climate of respect for moral behaviour. The extra commandment in most moral systems is, 'Thou shalt not be found out', but even this type of hypocrisy is the homage that immorality pays to morality. We could admit all the crimes of religion, acknowledge the hypocrisy and guilt it creates, and still believe there is a vital connection between religion and moral aspiration. Many religious leaders will say, for instance, that we are still living off the moral capital invested by Christianity in its hey-day. Christian ethics, it is claimed, are intrinsically connected to, and an expression of, Christian doctrine. It is acknowledged that many people go on affirming and trying to practise the ethic even after they have abandoned the doctrines associated with it. That state of affairs cannot continue for long, they warn us. The ethical investment inherited from the doctrinal system will soon be used up and we shall then descend into immorality and ethical confusion. The implication of this warning is that we must re-invest in the doctrines that underpin the ethic if we want the ethic back. But there are several difficulties with this. People of integrity are unlikely to be able to persuade themselves of the truth of religious claims simply because they acknowledge that these can have certain beneficial side-effects. Let us leave on one side for the moment whether the side-effects are all that beneficial and stick to the point at issue: even if a religious connection to a good ethic is established, is it always necessary to accept the religion in order to have the ethic? Can the ethic not stand on its own as something that is likely to commend itself to people who want to try to live well and believe in the importance of morality for healthy human communities? When we think about it, there appears to be something unprincipled about asking people to adopt religion because it helps them to behave well and not because it is true. Of course, religious leaders rarely suggest this, but there is often a kind of incoherence in the approach they do adopt. They insist on a connection between religious decline and ethical confusion, and most observers would probably accept that there is, indeed, a connection. It is where we go from that connection that is of interest to me and is the purpose behind this book.

If I refrain from physically and mentally abusing my wife, because my religion persuades me that wife abusers will burn eternally in hell, then we could say that the religious belief is having a beneficial effect, however irrational the belief itself may be. If I abandon my belief in eternal punishment (the religious doctrine that has previously put a restraint on my violence) and start beating my wife again, it seems morally bankrupt to argue that the only way to correct me is by persuading me of the truth of something that seems intrinsically unbelievable and, in its own way, morally dubious. In other words, it might be possible to accept the connection between the abandonment of a belief and the resumption of bad behaviour, and still believe that we can make a case for the good moral behaviour unconnected to the previously held belief.

We could also argue that issues of truth are themselves moral issues. If we have become persuaded that a particular claim is not true or is one we can no longer hold with a clear conscience, then we are making a moral judgement; we are saying that it is important to act on what we believe to be true and not cling to falsehoods because they comfort us or because they have beneficial secondary effects. It is in this area that we come close to the exasperation that many people who aspire to live moral lives feel towards religion. They understand the historical connection between religion and ethics, though that connection, for them, is no longer vital or logical. They would tell us that it is important for them to have a proper sense of responsibility towards others, which, if it is no longer anchored to religion, must find an anchor somewhere else, possibly in humanity itself.

In other words, just because the connection between ethics and religion has been broken, it does not follow that it is no longer possible to have ethics. It may mean that we have to discover and promote the importance of a non-religious ethic. And such an ethic could be a genuinely ecumenical ethic that appealed, in its broad principles, to people who were religious and to people without religion, to people who believed in God and to people who did not. Unless it is more important to believe that wife beaters go to hell than to stop wife beating itself, religious believers will be able to support an ethic that achieved or sought to achieve the same end, the ending of wife abuse.

Another difficulty with religion and ethics is the way religions tend to associate God with particular stages or phases in social development. Various examples will be adduced in this book, but the most eloquent and obvious one has been the varying status of women in the history of Christianity. It is one thing to recognise that gender relations reflect historical and social realities; it is another to claim that they have been permanently established by God in a specific pattern. If we claim the latter, the legitimate critique made by feminists against male dominance and oppression has to be made against God. We either admit that God is, to some extent at least, a human construct that is subject to criticism and evolution, or we weld religion to unsustainable prejudices that guarantee its rejection for the best, not the worst of reasons, so that to abandon it becomes a virtuous act of revolt against an oppressive force that imprisons rather than liberates humanity.

This book is not about God and whether God *exists*, but it does rest on a belief that we must disconnect religion and God from the struggle to recover some elements of a common ethic. To that extent, therefore, this is a godless

book, but discerning readers will detect a paradox at work.
If there is that which we call God, and God is more than the
projection of our own best values and longings for trans-
cendence, then God must be involved in all our moral
struggles, so the attempt by humans to discover a morality
apart from God might, paradoxically, be God's greatest
triumph; and our attempt to live morally as though there
were no God might be the final test of faith. There will be
frequent references to God and religion in this book, but the
aim is to unite those who believe with those who do not in
the discovery of a workable ethic for our time. Before
embarking on that exploration, however, we need to
establish some distinctions between religious attitudes to
human behaviour and the purely ethical approach I want to
put forward in this book.

There is an important distinction between sin and immorality. Sin is an essentially religious idea; an ancient
definition describes it as disobedience of God. One way of
thinking about this is to see it against the patriarchal
background of Christianity, which thought of God as a
father with a strict code for the upbringing of his children.
In this particular father's house are many rules and regula-
tions, many activities that are forbidden, many that are
required. There may be an undisclosed rational ground for
these prohibitions and imperatives, but the concept of sin
essentially works on the basis of obedience rather than
consent, blindly following what is commanded, rather than
co-operating with an end that is understood and voluntarily
accepted. Indeed, there are passages in the Bible where God
orders the performance of acts of great wickedness in order
to test the obedience of his children. The most extreme test
is found in Genesis chapter 22, where Abraham's obedience
is tested by God in a particularly cruel way:

After these things God tested Abraham. He said to him, 'Abraham!' And he said, 'Here I am.' He said, 'Take your son, your only son Isaac, whom you love, and go to the land of Moriah, and offer him there as a burnt offering on one of the mountains that I shall show you.' So Abraham rose early in the morning, saddled his donkey, and took two of his young men with him, and his son Isaac; he cut the wood for the burnt offering, and set out and went to the place in the distance that God had shown him. On the third day Abraham looked up and saw the place far away. Then Abraham said to his young men, 'Stay here with the donkey; the boy and I will go over there; we will worship, and then we will come back to you.' Abraham took the wood of the burnt offering and laid it on his son Isaac, and he himself carried the fire and the knife. So the two of them walked on together. Isaac said to his father Abraham, 'Father!' And he said, 'Here I am, my son.' He said, 'The fire and the wood are here, but where is the lamb for a burnt offering?' Abraham said, 'God himself will provide the lamb for a burnt offering, my son.' So the two of them walked on together.

When they came to the place that God had shown him, Abraham built an altar there and laid the wood in order. He bound his son Isaac, and laid him on the altar, on top of the wood. Then Abraham reached out his hand and took the knife to kill his son. But the angel of the Lord called to him from heaven, and said, 'Abraham, Abraham!' And he said, 'Here I am.' He said, 'Do not lay your hand on the boy or do anything to him; for now I know that you fear God, since you have not withheld your son, your only son, from me.'

(NRSV Genesis 22.1–14)

This powerful and mysterious narrative is probably a remnant from a time when human sacrifice was practised, but this kind of historical approach dilutes its religious value by trying to account for the offence that is the very point of the story. The event celebrates the type of consciousness that wants to be commanded to perform extreme acts of obedience by an absolute authority whose attractiveness lies in its very refusal to explain itself. This is the heart of the concept of sin: sin is not only committing what is forbidden by God, but refusing to do what is commanded by God. The power of the concept lies in the unthinking nature of the obedience that is demanded.

It is easy to find a naturalistic explanation of the role of obedience in religion, and to see some of its expressions as fragmentary survivals of once complete systems that had meaning in a particular context. Human sacrifice, for instance, would make sense to a world-view that saw God as a tyrannous lord who demanded the best parts, the first fruits, of his serfs' labours. Most political systems have been structures of domination in which the vast majority of the population worked to support and provide comforts for a tiny elite. Human sacrifice seems to have been a part of religious systems in certain highly authoritarian cultures, and it is not difficult to follow its social logic in a society that was governed by a system of absolute obedience to a commanding power.

As social and religious systems change, codes and practices change with them, but the underlying notion of obedience to authority remains, though it is usually converted into a metaphor for loyalty to a relationship that has been freely adopted. The monarchy in Britain provides an example of the survival of a vocabulary that once applied absolutely in one context, and is now applied metaphorically in another. Though British monarchs no longer have the kind of power and authority they once had, the vocabulary of absolute power is preserved in documents and semantic style, so the people of Britain are still *subjects* not *citizens*, and the Queen *commands* her loyal subjects to appear at this or that event or to receive this or that privilege or responsibility. The form and vocabulary of a previous dispensation are retained long after they have lost any substantive meaning. A similar evolution occurs in religious traditions. However, the evolutionary or historical approach to these matters creates difficulties for those who retain traditional ideas of God. If we are prepared to admit that previous generations were wrong to believe that God wanted them to kill their children as a sacrifice, then we have already moved to a developmental or dynamic understanding of God and sin. We have also, more importantly, entered a fundamental protest against the concept of blind obedience itself, by stressing the importance of our own moral and rational assent to what is commanded. Once we do this, however, the concept of sin loses much of its power as an exercise of divine authority upon us.

When we ask whether it is right to obey a particular imperative that claims to be the will of God, we have asserted our own moral reasoning as a higher value than the simple acceptance of the alleged claims of divinity, mediated through religious traditions, because we are no longer able to accept many of the values expressed by these systems. We are not debating here whether anything is left of the idea of God as such, or whether God now has to be conceived as being within the moral struggle itself, in some sense prompting or engaging with us in the process. What many people have clearly departed from is any sense that the moral life, lived intentionally and consciously, is consistent with blind obedience to any authority, including what is alleged to be divine authority. The difficulty is not with the idea of obeying what is genuinely known to be a divine command: how could anyone who knew that a command was genuinely divine want to disobey it? The difficulty lies in the fact that history has taught us that many claims made on behalf of God have been subsequently rejected for moral reasons, so the fact that an injunction comes with a divine label attached is no guarantee of divine origin. We know that many of the systems that have used the concept of sin and unthinking obedience have been based upon structures of power and control, domination systems that have been intrinsically oppressive, so that the idea of sin itself was part of a mechanism of force designed to secure compliance to authority.

While the political origin of these systems is easy to understand, their metaphysical base is more difficult to uncover. The background seems to be some sort of dualism that divides the created reality from the heavenly sphere and posits creation as fallen by nature, intrinsically sinful, and in some kind of bondage to evil. Various redemption schemes are then proffered as ways of rescue from this bondage to creation. There are surviving elements of different kinds of rescue theology in the Bible, in both the Old and New Testaments, and the life and teaching of Jesus have been interpreted to fit them. Indeed, in some of the explanations of the death of Jesus there are echoes of the theme of sacrifice of the first-born son to appease an angry divinity. One theory of the death of Jesus clearly gets its emotional power from half-forgotten echoes of the ancient practice of human sacrifice. One of the lessons or prophecies in the ancient Christian Liturgy of Holy Saturday is the story of the sacrifice of Isaac, which we have already looked at, and the parallel is clear. Our salvation or rescue from the anger of God is purchased by the death of Jesus, God's own Son. God has to be bought off, if the whole human race is not to be damned, and who more fitting for such a sacrifice than the only begotten Son of God? Much of this way of thinking comes from a complex religion called Gnosticism, which based itself on the theory that the creation is the work, not of Almighty God, but of evil minor gods from whose clutches we must be rescued by secret knowledge and mysterious rites. The concept of sin is a powerful part of this anxious world-view, and it works by the energy of fear. In the Gospels Jesus attacked this system and, in its place, proclaimed unmediated access to God, whose kingdom is already in our midst, not at some eschatological distance to which we might attain if we get into the right salvation programme. So the good life is no longer a matter of avoiding a series of external and objective activities that are wrong in themselves; it is now a more subtle business of developing appropriate inner intentions, leading to love of and compassionate action towards our neighbours.

Redemption systems all suffer from various kinds of internal incoherence, as well as contradicting our current understanding of the nature of creation, but they continue to offer powerful emotional symbolism to people and they can be interpreted in ways that make creative use of their religious energy and imagery. Many people commit themselves to these systems, using the traditional vocabulary as a metaphor for human experience of bondage and fear, redemption and hope. Their effectiveness lies in the way they help people design their lives into patterns that rescue them from chaos and confusion. Several of these ancient, ritualised systems are still intact in many cultures and continue to provide safe enclosures for vulnerable humans. The most complete systems work by carefully organising life into a series of requirements and prohibitions in which dietary and sexual arrangements are all minutely prescribed. The modern expression of Gnosticism that is loosely described as New Age spirituality offers various current versions of such a ritualised life. In their rituals, New Agers borrow traditions from many sources and adapt them to their own style. Their effectiveness comes from the commitment that is brought to the system.

Whether we call it the placebo effect or human credulity, the fact remains that beliefs are powerful as long as they are believed. They have a stabilising effect on human anarchy and confusion, and bring order to disordered lives. It is for this reason that those of us who are unimpressed by the truth claims of traditionalist systems have to recognise that they do offer some people the kind of absolute and defining structure they need, if their lives are not to descend into chaos. Sometimes, for instance, drug addicts escape from their substance dependence into dependence on various versions of religious fundamentalism. It is easy to accuse them of substituting one kind of drug for another, but addiction to religion, while it might be boring for the rest of us to listen to, can save such lives from chaos and destruction. I know of one heroin addict who has recently been converted to a fundamentalist version of Christianity. His family rejoice in his freedom from drugs, but the price they pay is having to endure his relentless efforts to convert them from their mild attachment to Christianity to his newly discovered full-frontal fundamentalism. The power of all fundamentalisms lies in their persuasive effect, not in their truthfulness. As long as *belief* in their underlying truthfulness endures, there is both power and integrity in their claims. The crisis occurs when the systems remain intact on the surface long after they have been emptied of their primary metaphysical content. This accurately describes the cultural state of many religious systems in our own society, so it is not surprising that the vacuum created is filled by the kind of absolute systems that so characterise the scene today.

The dilemma for the liberal mind is how to balance its abhorrence of such intellectual slavery against its recognition that it may be the only way to rescue certain people from something worse. It is easy to understand why a young person with no hope in the world, unemployed, living in a sink-housing-estate, with no prospect of any kind of self-transcendence, escapes into hard drugs. In the ghettos of America these are precisely the kind of people who can be transformed by the absolutist appeal of the Black Moslem culture or some versions of fundamentalist Christianity. We find the same thing happening in the prisons of the USA and Britain, where a particular brand of evangelical Christianity is highly successful at converting inmates to a life-changing commitment to religion. The liberal mind will acknowledge these trends, however uneasily, much in the way that Marx understood the function of religion as a necessary drug for the suffering and afflicted masses.

In spite of these examples of systems that still use the concept of sin effectively, it is problematic in our post-traditional society. It belongs to a particular type of religious consciousness, usually one that is based on a theory of creation (and the matter of which it is composed) as being in a fallen or unclean state. This idea of the impurity of matter, its suspect nature, will be particularly important when we come to think more closely about why some natural substances or acts are held to be evil and dangerous in themselves, so that the moral focus is upon the material or the activity rather than upon the agent. The sin concept transfers itself mechanically to certain natural acts and substances that are held to be wrong because they are wrong, not because of any evidence that is offered to support the claim. The difficulty comes when we mix up ritual pieties with moral claims. Christians who derive some of their traditions from the Old Testament frequently fall into this confusion. They fail to distinguish between ritual and moral systems and use the word sin indifferently in both contexts. Jews and Moslems are aware of the difference between a ritual and a moral prohibition, but certain parts of the Christian tradition seem to have lost the distinction and have fallen into a major intellectual confusion in the process. Ritual prohibitions characterise and define certain traditional religious systems, such as Orthodox Judaism, but they are not believed to be part of some universal moral law that is laid upon all humankind. They are part of the particularity of a special tradition, a specific kind of piety, much in the way that certain religious orders in the Christian tradition take on extra works of piety and self-denial as a voluntary way of life. It is important, therefore, to distinguish between particular ritual pieties and universally applicable moral principles. I may abjure pork, because my religion holds it to be ritually unclean, but I cannot justify that claim morally, except on grounds that have nothing to do with pigs. We might argue that if I have committed myself to a religious system that requires me to promise not to eat pork and I do eat it, I have committed a wrong act; but the wrong lies in breaking the promise because, while eating pork is demonstrably harmless, breaking promises is demonstrably harmful. While the distinction between ritual sin and immorality is one that is officially recognised by the interpreters of the ritual systems themselves, there is an inevitable tendency to blur the distinction and to load cultic imperatives with ethical weight. The most significant of these confusions comes from the passage in Leviticus where it is written: 'You shall not lie with a male as with a woman; it is an abomination.' (18.22) The Hebrew word here translated 'abomination' does not usually signify something intrinsically evil, like rape or theft, but something which is ritually unclean for Jews, like eating pork or engaging in sexual intercourse during menstruation, both of which are forbidden in Leviticus. Christians have too easily transposed ritual into moral sin in their interpretation of the Bible, with fateful consequences for many people.

The attitude of Jesus to these matters provides us with a useful way of defining the difference between sin and morality. Jesus used the vocabulary of sin, but he refused its identification with the breaking of external codes and rules, its materialisation or ritualisation. Sin came from the selfish heart, the inescapable human tendency to organise reality to suit ourselves even when it harms others. His attitude to sin was more congruent with present-day understandings of morality than the religious systems based on external obedience.

Morality tries to base itself on observed consequences, not on beliefs, superstitions or preferences. A wrong act is one that manifestly harms others or their interests, or violates their rights or causes injustice. There are many distinctions to observe here, and many calculations or approximations to be judged, but the central stream of the concept of wronging or harming another is reasonably clear. For instance, while I do not believe it is wrong to eat pork or drink alcohol, in the presence of a Moslem, moral courtesy would oblige me to abstain, just as it would oblige me to remove my shoes on entering a mosque. Though these are matters of moral indifference to me, I will try not to harm my Moslem neighbour's sensitivities while I am in his company by following these courtesies. On the other hand, if I found myself among a group of people who ritually killed convicted criminals during their great festival and I, as an honoured guest, was invited to make the first kill, not even courtesy to my uncomprehending hosts could persuade me to commit an act that so clearly violates a basic moral principle. For the idea of harm to work as a moral as opposed to a religious principle, we have to be able to give proof of the harm. Religious teachers might claim, for instance, that an act that had no harmful consequences discernible on earth was, nevertheless, forbidden by God and would be punished after death, so that the concept of harm was extended eschatologically and was therefore beyond human proving. Claims of this sort, while they may persuade religious people, do not sustain themselves by the kind of argument needed to justify human moral systems. Saying that an act is wrong, because it is forbidden by God, is not sufficient unless we can also justify it on moral grounds.

This is why debating with religious people about the morality or immorality of certain activities can be frustrating. If they tell us that a particular kind of sexual act, such as masturbation, is harmful, without being able to tell us why, they move from the realm of moral to religious discourse, thereby making moral negotiation impossible. If they tell us, however, that God forbids masturbation, because it makes its practitioners blind or causes hairs to grow upon the palms of their hands, we can verify or falsify these claims through experiment and observation. Religious moralists, in practice, usually flit between empirical and absolute justifications for their assertions, moving from the former to the latter when the argument is going against them. If we can use the idea of harm as our moral criterion, we will probably be drawn to admit that no act of consensual sex between responsible adults is immoral because of the sexual act itself, though it may be on other grounds. This is the basis, for instance, for the almost universal condemnation of adultery, as a betrayal of trust and the violation of a promise freely given. Even here there can be exceptions that prove the rule, such as the case of the man who had been faithfully married to his wife for thirty years when she contracted Alzheimer's disease. He continued to nurse her faithfully, though she had long since gone into that far country that is the tragic fate of those who suffer from this disease. Some years later he and a family friend, who assisted him in the arduous care of his wife, became lovers. Together they strengthened one another in their care for the woman they were theoretically sinning against. Was any actual harm committed here, except in the purely formal sense? This is an example of the way in which genuinely good things can be in conflict with one another, so that mature people try to learn to live with contradictions rather than insisting on neat resolutions.

Our search for basic moral principles, if we are wise, will always allow for situational variations of this sort. Morality is as much an art as a science and it calls for a certain versatility from us, the ability to improvise and respond to actual circumstances and particular situations. The difficulty that faces us today is that we have moved into a state where no single moral system has universal or even widespread appeal. This situation of moral pluralism is not at all the same thing as absolute moral relativism. We can acknowledge and even celebrate the fact of different moral systems, without falling into the trap of believing there are no moral principles that help us to define what it means to be human. The challenge that faces us is to separate the basic principles that might help to guide us through what has been called the moral maze from the kind of absolute systems that

claim to know the right answer to every moral dilemma
that faces us. Our era is characterised by discordant voices
and competing claims, all asserting their right to teach the
rest of us how to live and what values to hold.

We have already noted the absolute way in which
religious systems have historically operated. By claiming
divine authority for their commandments and prohibitions,
with eternal punishment for those who disobey them,
religious moral systems operate on the basis of fear. Fear
is a potent motivator of behaviour, and any civilly organised
society will acknowledge its importance in deterring and
punishing certain kinds of unacceptable conduct, but the
most effective systems will generally operate on the basis of
consent, not coercion; voluntary acceptance, not imposed
obedience. It is sometimes said that this is too feeble a
principle to impose order upon the unruly wills and desires
of sinful humanity, and that what is needed is an absolute
system that will put fear into people and scare them into
moral probity. The difficulty for this sort of claim is that we
have moved away from the world-view that gave it power.
Lies and illusions can have enormous power over us,
sometimes benignly, but they only work as long as they
are believed. Today, most of us do not believe in eternal
punishment for temporal mistakes. Nevertheless, we need
some kind of moral cohesion if we are not just to disintegrate into endless moral combat with no divine referee to
adjudicate rival claims. God no longer seems to provide the
kind of cohesion we need, because the systems that claimed
divine authorisation made some claims that we have subsequently repudiated for good reason. It is the cruelty of the
sanctions used against offenders in the traditional moral
systems that we find most revolting today. We are in the
interesting moral position of asserting certain of our own

values as higher than the ones allegedly associated with the divine will and its anger against sinners. It is also fairly clear to anyone with even a superficial understanding of the history of divinely mandated moral systems that they always bear a striking resemblance to, and offer confirmation of, the social systems in which they emerged. Just as it has been recognised that history is written by the winners, so we ought to acknowledge that they tend to write the moral systems as well. This should not surprise us. Even if we believed that we were responding in some way to the pressure of a transcendent mind and purpose upon our own time-bound nature, the divine will would still have to be exerted through the limiting reality of our own circumstances. Inevitably, the outworking of this moral imperative would be projected by us onto systems we ourselves would create.

For moral systems to work, we have to accord them some kind of authority over us. The dilemma is that they then work too well, so that reforming them becomes difficult. But this, paradoxically, is a sign of their effectiveness. If they could be overturned without much of a struggle, they would lack the very authority they need if they are to condition us into some kind of conformity. Moral change is always bound to be contentious, though it seems to characterise human history. There are always those who defend the status quo, because it provides stability and continuity, and there are always those who push against it, because they experience it as morally stunting and imprisoning. The biblical shorthand for this tension is the struggle between priest and prophet, priests being those who sanctify and defend what the community has heard God say in the past, while prophets are those who challenge the community to hear the new word God is saying in the present. The prophetic role is always un-comfortable and sometimes dangerous. But it is never a matter of simple moral evolution in one direction.

One of the things that will emerge in this book is the fact that good moral systems frequently compete and conflict with one another, so that there is an essentially tragic side to our search for values. I have already alluded to one way of defining that tension, in the struggle between the priestly and essentially conservative consciousness that is anxious to preserve institutions and the stability they guarantee, and the prophetic or radical consciousness that is always aware of the way powerful institutions can oppress people and frustrate creative diversity and the embracing of new ideas. There are many other ways in which we could define the range of moral contrasts, such as the Appollonian and the Dionysian, or the Puritan and the Cavalier. Each of these ways of being human has its greatness, its appeal, and each has its shadow. Part of Nietzsche's great critique of Christianity was that it inculcated a slave morality of obedience to authority and denial of the life-force, in contrast to the heroic ethic of struggle and overcoming. There are virtues of austerity and there are virtues of extravagance; there is value in freedom and there is value in order; there are Protestant virtues and Catholic vices, and vice versa. We can even learn to admire moral systems we could never permit ourselves to follow. We may even rejoice when we see people embracing moral systems we could never ourselves embrace, because these systems give a coherence to their lives and because they sincerely believe them.

What some of us must contend for, however, is the inescapability as well as the value of pluralism and the impossibility of there being any infallible way of concluding the debate in favour of a single system. This is why the use of God in moral debate is so problematic as to be almost worthless. We can debate with one another as to whether this or that alleged claim genuinely emanated from God, but who can honestly adjudicate in such an Olympian dispute? That is why it is better to leave God out of the moral debate and find good human reasons for supporting the system or approach we advocate, without having recourse to divinely clinching arguments. We have to offer sensible approaches that will help us to pick our way through the moral maze that confronts us. This book is one attempt to do that. It is an attempt to offer a human-centred justification for a particular moral approach. It is a morality without God.

CHAPTER ONE

Ethical Jazz

Some years ago Rupert Hart Davis wrote a short memoir of his mother called, *The Arms of Time*. The title came from a poem by Charles Tennyson Turner about his return, as an adult, to the haunts of his childhood. This is how the poem ends:

> But I was warn'd. 'Regrets which are not
>   thrust
> Upon thee, seek not; for this sobbing
>   breeze
> Will but unman thee; thou art bold to
>   trust
> Thy woe-worn thoughts among these
>   roaring trees,
> And gleams of by-gone playgrounds – Is't
>   no crime
> To rush by night into the arms of Time?'

Rupert Hart-Davis's mother had led a colourful life and was far from being a conventional parent. Part of the motive behind his book was to find and become acquainted with the mother he had hardly known. In the event, an exercise in family archaeology turned into a love letter to his dead mother, a celebration of her turbulent life and a compassionate act of understanding. Contrary to the poet's warning, rushing into the arms of time became an act of healing for the author. I was reminded of the Hart-Davis book when I read *Every Secret Thing*, Gillian Slovo's biography of her parents, both remarkable people and martyrs in the long war against Apartheid in South Africa. They had lived in exile for years, organising armed resistance to the South African regime. Gillian Slovo's mother was assassinated by a letter bomb in 1982 and her father died of cancer shortly after the inauguration of the new South Africa. Gillian Slovo was never able to lose a feeling of resentment that the cause of freedom in South Africa was more important to her parents than their own children. When Nelson Mandela comforted her after her father's death, he admitted that the children of people, like him and Jo Slovo, who had given their lives to the cause, had suffered a kind of orphaning from which they would never really recover. The Slovo book is more uncomfortable reading than the Hart-Davis one, mainly because the author is more prepared to let her own pain show, as well as guilt at feeling hurt by the neglect of heroic parents who helped to bring hope and, finally, freedom to millions. During her research Gillian Slovo unearthed information about various love-affairs her parents had, and she describes the conflict and confusion the discovery produced in her. Ultimately, however, the book conveyed a sense of absolution and healing. Finally to know was to forgive. For Gillian Slovo and Rupert Hart-Davis, rushing back into the arms of time brought understanding, and understanding brought compassion and pride.

Both of these exercises in biography illustrate one of the major tensions in the study and practice of the moral life. Is morality a science or an art, a technique we can learn by mastering the rules and applications, or is it more like mapping a strange country by a process of exploration, trial and error? To change the analogy, is the moral life like playing from a fixed text, or is it closer to the improvisations of jazz? And where does the pressure to think about these matters come from? If we no longer believe it is simply a matter of offering obedience to a series of divine commandments that were laid down to govern every human eventuality, where does the ethical struggle rise from, why does it afflict us? And is it really as simple as certain protagonists make out?

A permanent aspect of the human moral struggle seems to be the need to praise and to blame, to single out certain types of conduct for condemnation and others for laudation. The obvious way to account for this side of things is to see it as a reinforcement technique, a well-known way of inculcating good practice by praise and averting bad practice by blame. It is the way we train children and dogs, it is a technique we apply to ourselves in all sorts of areas. Humans like to be praised, we need positive reinforcement, and we hate to be blamed or shamed, we dislike humiliation. We learn to apply these insights to all sorts of areas, most notably to the moral life. In a rough and ready sort of way, this is what newspapers do when they hunt out scandals among the rich and famous, the powerful and the notable in public life. If they unearth an example of what they deem to be unacceptable behaviour, they parade the shame of it before millions, much in the way our forebears shamed notorious sinners by putting them in the stocks to make them objects of public humiliation. This is a complicated phenomenon, because shaming those who have been caught doing something most people are interested in, or occasionally fantasise about, probably has more to do with our own guilty pleasure than any positive desire to reinforce good behaviour. This kind of public sanctimony is often excused on the grounds that, whatever the motive, it discourages misconduct and is a necessary hypocrisy. It is probably true that if you impose upon a people a harsh enough set of sanctions against what is deemed to be bad behaviour you will succeed in keeping most of them in line. But is scaring or shaming people away from certain kinds of behaviour the same thing as helping them to become moral agents? It seems more like training dogs by Pavlovian methods of positive and negative reinforcement than introducing people to the moral life.

What makes the simple act of shaming or blaming people complicated is the knowledge that they each had a specific history, and the more we know about it the easier it becomes to understand why they did what they did. Even if it still seems necessary to us to condemn certain kinds of behaviour, it becomes a more complex matter when we have to apply the condemnation, not to abstract actions, but to real people in actual situations. Actual, self-conscious moral behaviour, as opposed to simple obedience out of fear or strict training, is more complicated than we sometimes admit, because we are beginning to confront the ancient dilemma of human responsibility. Can people help what they get up to? Are we really free to act in a way that makes the moral life a chosen path, or are we all determined by forces beyond our control? We are not going to resolve this endlessly important debate, but meditating about it may help us to be more cautious about some of the claims we make about the moral life, without entirely abdicating our sense of moral responsibility. And another literary diversion might help us address the point.

The text in question is the remarkable book on the Bulger murder case, *As If*, by Blake Morrison. The horrifying abduction and murder of two-year-old Jamie Bulger outraged Britain, and the trial that followed was affected by the way the news media sensationalised the whole affair.

The Home Secretary of the time acted politically in his involvement with the trial and the sentence that followed it. The event gave rise to one of those bouts of moral panic that frequently afflict us, making it almost impossible for the young killers to receive the sort of treatment that was appropriate to children of their age, no matter how terrible their crime. Morrison's book, by a process of painstaking investigation, accompanied by an intense amount of self-examination, showed us that the killers of Jamie Bulger were themselves victims. The difference between the Bulger book and the other two is that at the end, while we understand more about the matter, there is no sense of absolution or healing, though we hope that the boy killers might yet have a chance to do something with lives that started so inauspiciously and reached such a horrifying climax so soon.

The point in all of this is the role of knowledge in understanding the predicaments that human beings find themselves in. It is always easier to rush to judgement about situations we know little or nothing about. Then we can judge the bare act that has outraged us and lynch the perpetrators, either physically or judicially. Once we start digging, however, once we start rushing into the arms of time, the whole business of morality becomes more complex in its particularities, even though we may still hold to our moral generalities. Personal reflection and self-examination, as well as the study of human nature through the biographies of others, shows us that we are largely, though not necessarily completely, determined by forces that are beyond our control. We acknowledge how formative the first few years of life are for our social and psychic development; we rarely acknowledge the formative influence of the early millennia in the development of our species and the conflict and tension they built permanently into our natures.

Nietzsche was convinced that our moral struggle is the result of humanity's sundering from its animal past. He said that all the instincts that do not discharge themselves outwardly *turn inwards*. They do not cease with the emergence of consciousness, but it is now hard and rarely possible to gratify them, so they look for new, subterranean satisfactions. He goes on: 'Enmity, cruelty, joy in persecuting, in attacking, in change, in destruction [and I'd want to add sexuality to that daunting list] – all this turned against the possessor of such instincts: that is the origin of the "bad conscience" . . . thus was inaugurated the worst and uncanniest illness, from which man has not to the present moment recovered, man's suffering from man, from himself . . . From now on man awakens an interest, as if with him something were announcing, preparing itself, as if man were not a goal but only a way, an episode, a bridge, a great promise.'[1] It is the emergence of human consciousness that makes it possible to choose the moral life. It is important to emphasise choice here, because without freedom there can be no moral life as such. We might inculcate certain types of behaviour by a process of sanctions and rewards, but morality in the sense in which I am using the term involves a process of consent or aspiration, an assent to the kind of conduct we describe as ethical. Before the emergence of Nietzsche's 'bad conscience', with human consciousness we would have behaved instinctively, unreflectively, in response to our programmed needs and fears. With the emergence of consciousness comes the possibility of reflection upon the consequence of our own actions. Conscience is a witness to the complexity of human agency and the constraints upon it, as well as to the longing for the freedom to choose an action for reasons other than the pressure of instinct or circumstance. Part of our anguish is caused by the tension between this longing for human freedom, the ability to choose our own actions on rational or moral grounds, and our actual experience of weakness and fallibility. Add to all that the influence of the surrounding environment, itself the cumulative result of the other factors, and we have a picture of humanity as conditioned by a kind of ineluctable necessity that both determines us and tortures us with remorse over the state we are in – 'created sicke, commanded to be sound', as Lord Greville put it.[2]

At this point I would like to return to the other difficult element in this discussion for believers; the role of God in the creation of moral systems. As we indicated in the introduction, one way of resolving the problem is to commit ourselves, by an act of will, to the belief that the particular moral system we espouse is the permanent expression of the mind of God, and that our role is one of simple surrender and obedience. The codes that are supposed to command our obedience are contained in ancient texts, such as the Bible, to which believers have been traditionally exhorted to submit. To make this response effective, however, we need to protect ourselves from the results of the historical study of ancient texts, one of the major and most successful intellectual enterprises of the last two hundred years. This kind of scientific study bases itself on the assumption of the human origin of the texts and traditions before it, and not upon any theory or conviction as to their divine origin. Nevertheless, it is possible both to believe in the *inspired* nature of the texts, to believe that they are revelatory in the sense that they carry valuable understandings and insights into the meaning of human life, and to be a scientific student of their history. We know, for example, that moral traditions always originate in a particular social and historical context in which they make direct sense, either as a response to what was perceived as a divine command or as a particular conception of human nature and its responsibilities. Our difficulty is that, while we have retained fragments of these ancient codes, they are now entirely divorced from the context that gave them their original meaning and within which alone we are able to judge and understand them.

Alasdair MacIntyre gives an interesting example of how difficult it is to make sense of such fragmented survivals from older moral traditions, unless we can be trained to see them through the eyes of anthropologists who are skilled at observing and interpreting other cultures.[3] He quotes Captain Cook's surprise at what he took to be the lax sexual habits of the Polynesians and his astonishment at the sharp contrast between that and the rigid prohibition they placed on men and women eating together. When he enquired why, he was told that it was taboo for men and women to eat together, though no *reason* was discovered behind the prohibition. MacIntyre suggests that this was because the Polynesians themselves no longer understood the word they were using, a suggestion reinforced by the fact that Kamehameha II abolished the taboos in Hawaii forty years later in 1819 without much protest.

An anthropologist examining the debate in the Christian community today about the role of women and the possibility of ordaining them into the various ministerial hierarchies of the different churches would encounter similar taboos, though in this case various reasons are still offered for the prohibition. They usually centre round some theory of divine ordering of gender relations. Man has

authority over woman, one explanation claims, because
man represents the assertive, creative leadership of God,
whereas woman represents the passive receptivity of nature. Ancient biology assumed that women contributed
nothing except the hospitality of their wombs to the
formation of new lives, which were perfectly and completely enclosed in the sperm of the male. While this explanation offers some kind of historical justification for the
ancient taboo against women, it is no longer one that
commends itself to most people today, because the
world-view of which the taboo was the spiritual expression
has been eroded by social change and its impact on gender
roles. This is why the ordination of women usually passes
off with remarkably little fuss in churches that have been
able to introduce it, in spite of the centuries in which it was
held to be taboo. The Christian taboo against women
holding sacred office, like the Polynesian taboo against
men and women eating together, made sense in a social
and religious context that had a precisely demarcated
understanding of gender roles, supported by reference to
sacred texts that were created as much to confirm the roles
as to account for them. When all that is left is the taboo
separated from the environment that gave it power and
meaning, it collapses. Thereafter appeals to the tradition,
simply because it is tradition, no longer persuade.

This is why the appeal to tradition as an argument is
usually doomed to failure. By the time we start appealing to
tradition, in order to preserve some custom or practice, its
days are clearly numbered, because traditions really only
work when they are legitimated by widespread consent.
Once we start appealing to the past as argument we are
being false to the past itself, because we have removed it
from the circumstances that gave it logic and integrity and

have started recasting it to suit our own very different needs. Traditions work by unconscious acceptance. While they are effectively and unreflectively fulfilling their role, they continue to have one. Once they have to be appealed to as a clincher in an argument, we can be certain they have lost their role or are in the process of losing it. This does not mean, however, that it is impossible for traditions to evolve into new uses. Prudent historical institutions maintain themselves by a process of adaptation to changing circumstances. There is a profound instinct in us to maintain the historical continuity of our institutions, but there is also a constant need for adaptive adjustment to new knowledge and the changes it brings. Many of the most significant changes to our values and ideas can be cloaked and obscured by the apparent continuity of the institutions that carry them through history.

If the erosion of tradition is one of the main ingredients in the moral confusion of our time, the other is the crisis of authority. Many of the institutions, such as the Church, that once exerted real authority over us have seen their powers gradually diminish during this century. They may appear to be unaltered in style and culture, but they have largely lost their power to compel us. In the past, traditional authorities operated a system of moral commandment enforced by severe sanctions: thieves had their hands amputated, adulterers were buried alive, blasphemers were stoned to death, traitors were beheaded. Later, when the sanctions grew more tender, they were replaced by shame and social banishment, but they were still powerfully enforced by social stigma. The intrusions of tabloid newspapers are all that is left of these mechanisms of shame that are the remnants of once dominant command systems. Just as highly centralised command economic systems, such as

Soviet Russia, have been almost universally replaced by free market systems, so command moralities are gradually being replaced by systems of private choice, with resulting instability and anxiety. The institutions that claim to represent God, when they are not ignored altogether, are treated like other human institutions that have to earn their right to a hearing by the value of what they say, and not by virtue of who is saying it. Today, authority has to earn respect by the intrinsic value of what it says, not by the force of its imposition. There is a loss in this situation, of course, because power transitions are always dangerously unstable periods in human history, but there is unlikely to be a wholesale return to the past and its values unless we are overtaken by a mass religious movement that obliterates the radically plural nature of contemporary society. Barring that unlikely eventuality, we must do what we can to construct moral agreements that will have the authority of our reason and the discipline of our consent.

It is not yet obvious to anyone today what the basis for a new moral understanding might be. In subsequent chapters I shall offer a few suggestions for a way forward that will, paradoxically, return to a tradition earlier than the one from which we are emerging. What seems to be obvious today, however, is the disintegration of the old standards, with little that we can confidently put in their place. We could illustrate this theme in human history from almost any period, but it is probably true that our own time is characterised by an almost uniquely turbulent assault upon tradition. I think we can take comfort from several things. First of all, we are learning that moral traditions are human creations, usually in response to particular circumstances and their challenges. We are also beginning to recognise that the process of their formation has always been more

dynamic than we have sometimes been prepared to acknowledge, and the solidifying of the tradition at any
particular point, though desirable for the sake of stability,
is unavoidably arbitrary. It would seem to follow that we
can do again what we have done before, though with more
modesty and a greater sense of the provisionality of human
traditions. We are also recognising that human freedom is
more frail and difficult to measure than we have sometimes
been prepared to admit. This has several effects on moral
traditions, but one we ought to recognise is that the strong
and powerful will almost certainly have a disproportionate
role in the creating and policing of norms. Powerful groups
always create a distorting effect on human arrangements. A
moment's thought about the role of women in history, or
the place of gay people today, will illustrate the claim. All of
this should serve to make our moral explorations more
open to critical analysis and self-examination.

What this suggests, therefore, is the responsible but
exciting possibility of rethinking morality for our own
day, acknowledging our situation, its confusions and insights, while also recognising that we need order and
balance in our lives. But today, perhaps for the first time,
we shall struggle to achieve a morality that is self-imposed
and consented to by our own reasons, though even that will
not guarantee our compliance. Moral failure will continue
to characterise us, but it will be an improvement if we can at
least consent to the tradition we are breaking. We shall
recognise that the creation of morality is our business, it is
something we have to do for our own sake if we are to live
sanely and with care for one another and the good of
society. We will try to avoid the panic that forces us into the
false belief that ours is a uniquely confused, perhaps
uniquely evil, generation. There can be little dispute about

the awfulness of human behaviour in the century that is drawing to a close, scarred as it has been by some acts of evil that are unique in their scale, if not in their quality. We could easily stampede ourselves into a refusal to look steadily at the complexities that confront us and take refuge in some irrecoverable, imagined past, forgetting that in that past are some of the most horrifying crimes of our history.

Command moralities may exercise a nostalgic appeal in a time of such confusion. A second look at them ought to discourage us from trying to replicate them today. Whatever other characteristics the emerging morality must have, it must be characterised by the principle of consent. We no longer live in command societies in which we instinctively obey orders from above, wherever above is thought to be. For better or for worse, we live in an age in which justifications have to be offered for moral restraints upon individuals. But we also live in an era where it is recognised that restraint is a necessary discipline for a fully human and sustainable existence. Part of the recovery of a common morality will involve us in a process of demythologising previous moral traditions; and part of it will involve us in the painstaking construction of new traditions. This activity is one of the things that defines us as human, so we should be exhilarated rather than depressed by the prospect.

If we reject the role of God as a micromanager of human morality, dictating specific systems that constantly wear out and leave us with theological problems when we want to abandon them, we shall have to develop a more dynamic understanding of God as one who accompanies creation in its evolving story like a pianist in a silent movie. We can opt for a series of fixed texts that wear out and have to be constantly changed, or we can choose the metaphor of the jazz session that constantly makes new music by listening to what's happening around it and applying the best of what is left of the tradition to the current context. The genius of improvisation seems to be a better metaphor for actual human moral experience than struggling to apply a single text to every situation. God invites us to join in the music, to listen and adapt to one another, to keep the melody flowing. Part of this versatility will involve us in listening to and respecting themes we ourselves do not choose to follow; and part of it will encourage us to find common themes in which many of us can participate. One of the intentions behind this book is to develop some of these common themes and explore the possibility of a new moral ecumenism that would unite people on the basis of an agreed human ethic.

CHAPTER TWO

Unhappy Bedfellows

This chapter will be mainly about sex, but I am not sure whether to start with philosophy or poetry, with Schopenhauer or Betjeman. Poets, after all, have written more about sex than philosophers have. In fact, Schopenhauer is the only major philosopher to have addressed the subject, apart from Plato, who, as Schopenhauer dismissively observed, confined his discussion 'to the sphere of myths, fables, and jokes, and for the most part concerns only the Greek love of boys'.[1] Schopenhauer does not seem to have had a strong sense of humour, so I suspect he missed some of the point in Plato, and sex is such a baffling subject that 'myths, fables and jokes' constitute as good an approach as any other. Nevertheless, it is probably true that Schopenhauer's section on The Metaphysics of Sexual Love in his master work, *The World as Will and as Representation*, is the first purely philosophical approach on offer. Even so, I am reluctant to start there, because it would be too earnest an introduction to a subject that is daunting enough. So I'll start with poetry, but not yet with Betjeman, though we'll come to him in a minute.

Shakespeare said just about everything that could be said on the subject of the complexity of human sexual relationships. We get from him a compassionate view, a strong sense of the helplessness of humanity before this powerful force. It is true he chronicles the comic follies and delusions of love, as well as its tragic cost, but we have to remember that he was not only the great genius who observed with sorrow and love the antics of the poor human player thrust upon the stage of life, he was himself touched with our infirmities. He, too, was a lover, and one of the best places from which to begin an exploration of the ethics of human sexuality is that exasperated cry in Sonnet 129.

> The expense of spirit in a waste of shame
> Is lust in action; and till action, lust
> Is perjur'd, murderous, bloody, full of blame,
> Savage, extreme, rude, cruel, not to trust;
> Enjoyed no sooner but despised straight;
> Past reason hunted; and no sooner had,
> Past reason hated, as a swallow'd bait,
> On purpose laid to make the taker mad;
> Mad in pursuit, and in possession so;
> Had, having, and in quest to have, extreme;
> A bliss in proof, – and prov'd, a very woe;
> Before, a joy propos'd; behind, a dream.
>> All this the world well knows; yet none knows well:
>> To shun the heaven that leads men to this hell.

Schopenhauer does not quote this sonnet, but he would have approved the sense of powerful irrationality it radiates, the sense that we are in the grip of a force we cannot control, that is indifferent to our happiness and is interested only in its own ends. We shall see what philosophy makes of it in a minute, but let us turn to Betjeman to capture a more wistful, less damning note. In a celebrated television interview at the end of his life, sitting in a wheel chair, wrapped up against a chill Cornish wind, Betjeman was asked what he regretted most about his life: 'Not having more sex,' he replied. One got a sense of someone who had denied himself the pleasures of sexual love for abstract, probably religious reasons, looking back and wondering what all the fuss had been about and whether the denial had been worth it. Certainly, he was brilliant at capturing the longings of innocent lust, those heart-stabbing moments of awareness when we are pierced with desires that come upon us like sorrow. Here's my favourite. It's called, wistfully, 'Senex'.

> Oh would I could subdue the flesh
> Which sadly troubles me!
> And then perhaps could view the flesh
> As though I never knew the flesh
> And merry misery.
>
> To see the golden hiking girl
> With wind about her hair,
> The tennis-playing, biking girl,
> The wholly-to-my-liking girl,
> To see and not to care.
>
> At sundown on my tricycle
> I tour the Borough's edge,
> And icy as an icicle
> See bicycle by bicycle
> Stacked waiting in the hedge.
>
> Get down from me! I thunder there,
> You spaniels! Shut your jaws!
> Your teeth are stuffed with underwear,
> Suspenders torn asunder there
> And buttocks in your paws!
>
> Oh whip the dogs away my Lord,
> They make me ill with lust.
> Bend bare knees down to pray, my Lord,
> Teach sulky lips to say, my Lord,
> That flaxen hair is dust.

Betjeman was a kind man, so there is compassion in what he calls his 'merry misery' over sex. He was struggling with desire and its confusions, but the struggle did not turn ugly; he did not, like many ascetics, become a hater, the kind of man who condemns in others what he struggles with in his own nature. That's the religious inversion, the root of the sexual pessimism that so disfigures the history of Christianity. Betjeman was in touch with his desires, had pity for them, though he tried to make them go away, by resorting to the prayer of detachment: *Teach sulky lips to say, my Lord, That flaxen hair is dust.* Of course, he knew well that it is the very transience of the objects of our love that most moves and compels us, because we are reaching through them to a permanence that escapes us at the very moment of possession.

Part of the trouble with human sexuality is that it is itself and something else at the same time. When we discussed humanity's bad conscience in the previous chapter, we noted that our dilemma is created by the conflict between nature and human consciousness, so that actions which in our animal past would have been followed unreflectively are now complicated by our own awareness of what we are doing. A partial analogy is being in the driving seat of a runaway car whose brakes have failed while descending a steep hill. We know that if we were in complete control of the situation with a fully functioning vehicle there would be a number of routines we could follow that would slow the car or bring it to a halt. Some of the systems *are* working, so we have partial control of the situation, but there are a number of unpredictable elements over which we have no control, such as a damaged brake system. Human sexuality often feels like a runaway car. We know what a destructive force it can be, we even know what it would take to direct it wisely, but the human community is never completely in control of it. We cannot simply let it rush headlong in any direction it chooses, but the methods of control available to us are by no means infallible, and they are subject to all sorts of unpredictable factors. One of the most powerful and unpredictable aspects of the sexual urge is its romantic or emotional dynamic. We become emotionally involved with the objects of our desire, fixated upon them, obsessed. This connection between sexuality and romantic longing for the other person means that sex itself can become a symbol for other kinds of union, the longing to merge or lose ourselves in the beloved. This is why the great mystics often chose the language of desire and sexuality to describe the soul's longing for God and the transcendent. It is this duality that makes sexuality so fascinating. If it were simply a basic need to perform an obvious bodily function, it might continue to fascinate, delight or captivate us, the way food and drink do, but it would no longer ensnare us in the delusion that, if we could only make the right connection this time, it would transform life itself and give it a transcendent new meaning. And that provides us with a convenient way of returning to Arthur Schopenhauer.

It is very easy to fault Schopenhauer on the detail of his analysis, to be irritated or amused by his fussier opinions, but he seems to have got to the heart of the problem with great clarity. What draws two individuals together, he claims, is the will-to-live of the whole species. In order to do this, nature attains her aim by planting in individuals a certain delusion, so that what in truth is merely a good thing for the *species* seems to the lovers to be a good thing for *themselves*. They serve the species under the delusion that they are serving themselves. He writes: 'In this process a mere chimera, which vanishes immediately afterwards, floats before him, and, as motive, takes the place of a reality. This delusion is instinct. In the great majority of cases, instinct is to be regarded as the sense of the species which presents to the will what is useful to it.'[2] So sexual love is a necessary ruse practised upon individuals by the species in order to ensure the life of the whole. It is here that Schopenhauer comes closest to the Shakespeare of Sonnet 129.

> *Everyone who is in love will experience an extraordinary dis-illusionment after the pleasure he finally attains; and he will be astonished that what was desired with such longing achieves nothing more than what every other sexual satisfaction achieves, so that he does not see himself very much benefited by it. That desire was related to all his other desires as the species is to the individual, hence as the infinite to something finite. On the other hand, the satisfaction is really for the benefit only of the species, and so does not enter into the consciousness of the individual, who, inspired by the will of the species, here served with every kind of sacrifice a purpose that was not his own at all. Therefore, after the consummation of the great work, everyone who is in love finds himself duped; for the delusion by means of which the individual was the dupe of the species has disappeared.*[3]

If we find this unduly pessimistic, we ought to reflect for a moment on the intoxicating madness of being-in-love, that state of idealised projection when we do not see the beloved as others see her, but only in the light of the magic delusion itself. That is why Schopenhauer believed that friendship rather than passion was a better basis for marriage, and we would probably all agree, but who would want to live completely without passion? Well, as we shall see, lots of people would, precisely because they do not like abandoning control, no matter what the will-to-live of the species

might be. But passion needs no recruiting agent. It dom-
inates the headlines, making fools of the great and the good,
breaking hearts, damaging lives, distorting the judgement of
good people, prompting them to irrational actions and
reckless affairs that destroy their own peace, so that, in
Saint Paul's words, they no longer understand their own
actions, for the good that they would they do not, while the
folly they would avoid they plunge headlong into. In a
purple passage Schopenhauer offers us an insight that
deconstructs the poetry of love, telling us that the longings
of lovers

> are the sighs of the spirit of the species, which sees here, to be won
> or lost, an irreplaceable means to its ends, and therefore groans
> deeply. The species alone has infinite life, and is therefore capable
> of infinite desire, infinite satisfaction, and infinite sufferings. But
> these are here imprisoned in the narrow breast of a mortal; no
> wonder, therefore, when such a breast seems ready to burst, and
> can find no expression for the intimation of infinite rapture or
> infinite pain with which it is filled. This, then, affords the
> material for all erotic poetry of the sublime kind, which accord-
> ingly rises into transcendent metaphors that soar above all that is
> earthly.[4]

He tells us that the species wages war with individuals and
their moralities. It knows no morality except its own will-to-
live, so that it has no scruple about over-riding our happiness and well-being, because the species has a closer and
prior right to us than the individual has.[5] This was why the
Romans personified the genius of the species as Cupid, from
the Latin for passion or desire. Cupid was a malevolent,
cruel, and ill-reputed god, in spite of his childish appearance;
he was a capricious, despotic demon, whose attributes were
a deadly dart, blindness and wings. Cupid's arrows strike us

with desires that are blind not only to the actuality of the beloved, whom we observe through a haze of delight and longing, but to the consequences for our own peace of mind and heart. Cupid cares for none of these things, cares nothing for us; he does his work and flies away.

This account of the power of our sexuality fits well with Nietzsche's understanding of the human predicament as a consequence of humanity's sundering from its animal past. If the species did its relentless work only through unconscious creatures, animals, there would be no moral anguish, no moral struggle, there would simply be the life-force, the will-to-live of Schopenhauer, relentlessly expressing itself. In us, however, that process has become conscious, has started observing itself, has, in Nietzsche's words, given itself a bad conscience. And this is the origin of morality, this need to find some kind of balance between instinctive and intentional life, between the drive of the species and the consciousness of the individual. I suspect that our longing for some kind of contentment and control is at the root of the invention of sexual morality. We recognise that living unintentionally, letting old Cupid have his way with us without resistance, breeds tragedy as well as joy, pain as well as pleasure. This is why all cultures develop some kind of sexual ethic.

The important thing to notice here, particularly when we come to think about the Christian angle on sexuality, is that in most cultures the sexual act is seen as morally neutral in itself, so the problem lies not with sex as such but with its tendency to excess and disorder. In Michel Foucault's unfinished history of sexuality much light is thrown upon the differences and similarities between classical Greek thought and Christian doctrine.[6] In the later Christian attitude to the flesh, sexual pleasure was itself the root of evil, because it derived its force from the Fall of Adam and Eve and was the mechanism that transmitted original sin. For some of the early Christian Fathers, sex would not have been a pleasure, and therefore not a problem, before the Fall. Adam and Eve would have conjugated without passion, if the serpent had not tempted the first woman to eat of the forbidden fruit. There are myths in other cultures that try to account for the force and variety of sexual attraction, but the developed Christian understanding of the myth of the Fall is distinctive, because it renders sex problematic in itself. It might be useful to compare it to the need to eat, for instance. It is obvious that eating can become a modality that expresses various kinds of human pathology. Some people eat to excess; some people suffer from complex eating disorders; some people use eating as an emotional substitute or compensation. Most of us would accept the need for some kind of ethic of eating, so that we could balance the importance of eating for health and survival with the dangers of eating the wrong thing or eating to excess or not eating enough. Part of that ethic would be an aesthetic of eating, if the popularity of cookery books and television programmes on the subject is anything to go by. We would not see eating as problematic in itself, though we would recognise that the human genius for pathologising nature applies here as well. The distinctive thing about the Christian ethic of sexuality is that, in one of its dominant forms, it sees the sex drive itself as uniquely constitutive of human sinfulness, as the very vehicle that transmits the virus of sin through history.

Now the serpent was more crafty than any other wild animal that the Lord God had made. He said to the woman, 'Did God say, "You shall not eat from any tree in the garden?"' The woman said to the serpent, 'We may eat of the fruit of the trees in the

*garden; but God said, "You shall not eat of the fruit of the tree
that is in the middle of the garden, nor shall you touch it, or you
shall die." ' But the serpent said to the woman, 'You will not die;
for God knows that when you eat of it your eyes will be opened,
and you will be like God, knowing good and evil.' So when the
woman saw that the tree was good for food, and that it was a
delight to the eyes, and that the tree was to be desired to make one
wise, she took of its fruit and ate; and she also gave some to her
husband, who was with her, and he ate. Then the eyes of both
were opened, and they knew that they were naked; and they
sewed fig leaves together and made loincloths for themselves.*

*They heard the sound of the Lord God walking in the garden at
the time of the evening breeze, and the man and his wife hid
themselves from the presence of the Lord God among the trees of the
garden. But the Lord God called to the man, and said to him,
'Where are you?' He said, 'I heard the sound of you in the garden,
and I was afraid, because I was naked; and I hid myself.' He said,
'Who told you that you were naked? Have you eaten from the tree
of which I commanded you not to eat?' The man said, 'The woman
whom you gave to be with me, she gave me fruit from the tree, and I
ate.' Then the Lord God said to the woman, 'What is this that you
have done?' The woman said, 'The serpent tricked me, and I ate.'
The Lord God said to the serpent,*

'Because you have done this,
   cursed are you among all animals
   and among all wild creatures;
upon your belly you shall go,
   and dust you shall eat
   all the days of your life.
I will put enmity between you and the woman,
   and between your offspring and hers;
he will strike your head,
   and you will strike his heel.'

To the woman he said,
  'I will greatly increase your pangs in childbearing;
  in pain you shall bring forth children,
yet your desire shall be for your husband,
  and he shall rule over you.'
And to the man he said,
  'Because you have listened to the voice of your wife,
  and have eaten of the tree
about which I commanded you,
  "You shall not eat of it,"
cursed is the ground because of you;
  in toil you shall eat of it all the days of your life;
thorns and thistles it shall bring forth for you;
  and you shall eat the plants of the field.
By the sweat of your face
  you shall eat bread
until you return to the ground,
  for out of it you were taken;
you are dust,
  and to dust you shall return.'

The man named his wife Eve, because she was the mother of all living. And the Lord God made garments of skins for the man and for his wife, and clothed them.

Then the Lord God said, 'See, the man has become like one of us, knowing good and evil; and now, he might reach out his hand and take also from the tree of life, and eat, and live forever' – therefore the Lord God sent him forth from the garden of Eden, to till the ground from which he was taken. He drove out the man; and at the east of the garden of Eden he placed the cherubim, and a sword flaming and turning to guard the way to the tree of life.

(NRSV Genesis 3.1-24)

It is here that we encounter one of these shifts in discourse and meaning that make debating about traditional religious insights so difficult. We have already referred to the way some of the early Christian commentators used the story of Adam and Eve and the fruit of the forbidden tree as a device to convey their particular view of sexuality. The trouble is that their account slides between history and myth, as Christian debate about sexuality and sin still does, so that it is difficult to know on what precise level we are debating. No educated, rational human can believe that Adam and Eve were historical figures or that the account of their ejection from the Garden of Eden, which contained a speaking serpent and a god who took evening walks, is anything other than a colourful folk tale or myth. It is undoubtedly a powerful myth that offers in narrative form a description of human relations that still carries meaning and truth for us today: but it is not history. To treat the myth as history and draw consequential deductions from it is intellectual sleight of hand or plain deception. We could exercise historical magnanimity and acknowledge how a generation that took the narrative as fact might be led to the kind of conclusions we have noted, but we ourselves would no longer treat them with anything other than anthropological tolerance. The trouble is that, in Christian thinking on the subject of sexuality, the power of this particular myth still affects attitudes as though we were dealing with a defining historical moment. It is this slipping and sliding between history and myth that makes debate about sexuality in some sections of Christianity so difficult. This is why we have to acknowledge that the Christian use of the myth of the Fall in the book of Genesis has been damaging to human self-understanding and has loaded us with a burden we are only beginning to shake off. It has built into Christian anthropology the crushing idea that, simply by being born, human beings inherit a sinful, fallen nature, like a congenital virus that can only be remedied by extraordinary methods.

More fatefully, it has held woman to be the primary agent of the Fall and the continuing means through which its deadly consequences are transmitted. This is all made brutally explicit in the *Malleus Maleficarum*, or '*Hammer of the Witches*', a handbook for inquisitors written by two Dominican friars in 1486. In the first part of their book the authors explain why women are more prone to witchcraft than men. They quote the book of Ecclesiasticus, chapter 25, on the inherent wickedness of women. 'Sin began with a woman, and because of her we all die. Do not leave a leaky cistern to drip or allow a worthless wife to say whatever she likes. If she does not accept your control, bring the marriage to an end.' (Ecclesiasticus, 25.24–26). Then they quote the famous mysoginistic rant of Saint John Chrysostom, Patriarch of Constantinople at the very end of the fourth century: 'What else is woman but a foe to friendship, an inescapable punishment, a necessary evil, a natural temptation, a desirable calamity, a domestic danger, a delectable detriment, an evil of nature painted with fair colours!' The authors note that, when they are talking about women in this way, they are really talking about sex, for which woman is a convenient metaphor. But after this momentary lapse into realism, their real fear and hatred of women bursts forth:

> *If the world would be rid of women, to say nothing of witchcraft, it would remain proof against innumerable dangers . . . I have found a woman more bitter than death . . . and as the sin of Eve would not have brought death to our souls and body unless the sin had afterward been passed to Adam, to which he was tempted by Eve, not by the devil, therefore is she more bitter than death. More bitter than death, again, because that is natural and destroys the*

body, but the sin which arose from woman destroys the soul by depriving it of grace, and delivers the body up to the punishment for sin. More bitter than death, again, because bodily death is an open and terrible enemy, but woman is a secret and wheedling enemy.

In case we have missed the point, they add:

All witchcraft comes from carnal lust, which in woman is insatiable.[7]

It is worth repeating that all of this comes from taking an ancient myth literally. It is a simple example of the way in which Christianity has allowed itself to be imprisoned by its own lack of historical imagination and versatility in interpreting ancient texts.

This poisonous nonsense is in marked contrast to the comparative sanity of the classical Greek understanding of sexuality. It is well-known that Christianity derived its most formative and important theological vocabulary from Greek philosophy. It also derived many of its ascetical practices from classical culture, as well as its passion for discipline and restraint; fatally, it informed the practice with a different motive. According to Foucault, for classical Greek thought, sexuality was potentially excessive by nature, so the moral question was how to control it, how to regulate its economy in an appropriate way. The regulated sexual economy was not achieved by a universal legislation that permitted or forbade certain acts, but rather by the achievement of an art of living that involved the individual in a battle to achieve dominion of the self over the self. This kind of self-overcoming was freely chosen for the sake of the self, just like any other discipline. It was not characterised by that particular anguish we find in the Christian struggle with sexuality, which loads it with such significance that it creates an ethic of anxiety and suspicion. The sexual act was not considered as a licit or illicit practice that had to be validated by certain external criteria. It was viewed as an activity that could be more or less pernicious in its consequences and should therefore be controlled and ordered. It was a practice that demanded reflection and prudence, so it was not so much a question of right and wrong as one of more or less.[8] This strikes me as such an obviously sane approach that I wonder why Christianity, which took so much from Greek thought, did not follow its usual practice here and lift the best that was going from the surrounding culture. What happened that caused Christianity to make such a fateful turning, and is it possible to rethink the whole subject?

To begin with, we have to exonerate the Bible. In the next chapter I shall make a plea for a more relaxed attitude to scripture and its authority for Christians, but it is only fair to point out that we probably read more into the Bible than we get out of it. There really is no single, discernible point of view to be found there, and what we do discover is often impossible to interpret, because we are so far from its original context. The Old Testament, like Homer and Shakespeare, mirrors its times and customs and does not seem to have any particular line on sex, as such, at all. Gradually, a priestly editorial line takes over that retrojects into the text an official interpretation of the earlier narratives, but the original material still sits there with its own primitive integrity intact. There are moving love stories and horrifying rapes, detailed descriptions of incest and matter-of-fact accounts of prostitution, tales of seduction and sexual revenge. Many types of relationship are recorded with a detachment that suggests that sex was accepted as a powerful reality that could certainly destroy harmony, but was itself no more morally problematic than the weather. Two examples that have proved embarrassing to later expositors will give us a sense of the matter-of-factness that characterises the approach of the Old Testament to human sexual experience. The first episode concerns Lot and his two daughters, after they have fled from the destruction of the cities of the plain, Sodom and Gomorrah.

> Now Lot went up out of Zoar and settled in the hills with his two daughters, for he was afraid to stay in Zoar; so he lived in a cave with his two daughters. And the firstborn said to the younger, 'Our father is old, and there is not a man on earth to come in to us after the manner of all the world. Come, let us make our father drink wine, and we will lie with him, so that we may preserve offspring through our father.' So they made their father drink wine that night; and the firstborn went in, and lay with her father; he did not know when she lay down or when she rose. On the next day, the firstborn said to the younger, 'Look, I lay last night with my father; let us make him drink wine tonight also; then you go in and lie with him, so that we may preserve offspring through our father.' So they made their father drink wine that night also; and the younger rose, and lay with him and he did not know when she lay down or when she rose. Thus both the daughters of Lot became pregnant by their father. The firstborn bore a son, and named him Moab; he is the ancestor of the Moabites to this day. The younger also bore a son and named him Benammi; he is the ancestor of the Ammonites to this day.

(NRSV Genesis 19.30–38)

Incest, for obvious reasons, is one of the most primitive taboos and it is sternly denounced later in the Old Testament, yet here we are offered a straightforward account of two unusual acts of incest that are motivated neither by lust nor by male power, but by the determination of two young women to preserve their father's line. The sexual content in the account is handled in an entirely matter-of-fact way, and it is this apparent indifference that was to embarrass later commentators. And the fact is that the Bible reserves a special role for the children born in that cave to two determined daughters of a drunken father. A Moabite woman called Ruth will marry an Israelite called Boaz, and their blood line will lead directly to the birth of David, the greatest of all the kings of Israel (Ruth 4.18–22). An Ammonite woman called Naamah will be one of Solomon's one thousand wives and concubines, and it is she who will give birth to Solomon's successor to the throne of Israel (I Kings 14.21). According to both the Jewish and the Christian traditions, it is from the House of David and Solomon that the Messiah will come.

The next story from the Old Testament is also an example of female determination, though in this case it describes a calculated act of prostitution that was designed to protect a woman's interests in a patriarchal society that placed unprotected women in a dangerous position.

It happened at that time that Judah went down from his brothers and settled near a certain Adullamite whose name was Hirah. There Judah saw the daughter of a certain Canaanite whose name was Shua; he married her and went in to her. She conceived and bore a son; and he named him Er. Again she conceived and bore a son whom she named Onan. Yet again she bore a son, and she named him Shelah. She was in Chezib when she bore him. Judah took a wife for Er his firstborn; her name was Tamar. But Er, Judah's firstborn, was wicked in the sight of the Lord, and the Lord put him to death. Then Judah said to Onan, 'Go in to your brother's wife, and perform the duty of a brother-in-law to her; raise up offspring for your brother.' But since Onan knew that the offspring would not be his, he spilled his semen on the ground whenever he went in to his brother's wife, so that he would not give offspring to his brother. What he did was displeasing in the sight of the Lord, and he put him to death also. Then Judah said to his daughter-in-law Tamar, 'Remain a widow in your father's house until my son Shelah grows up' – for he feared that he too would die, like his brothers. So Tamar went to live in her father's house.

In course of time the wife of Judah, Shua's daughter, died; when Judah's time of mourning was over, he went up to Timnah to his sheepshearers, he and his friend Hirah the Adullamite. When Tamar was told, 'Your father-in-law is going up to Timnah to shear his sheep,' she put off her widow's garments, put on a veil, wrapped herself up, and sat down at the entrance to Enaim, which is on the road to Timnah. She saw that Shelah was grown up, yet she had not been given to him in marriage. When Judah saw her, he thought her to be a prostitute, for she had covered her face. He went over to her at the road side and said, 'Come, let me come in to you,' for he did not know that she was his daughter-in-law. She said, 'What will you give me, that you may come in to me?' He answered, 'I will send you a kid from my flock.' And she said, 'Only if you give me a pledge, until you send it.' He said, 'What pledge shall I give you?' She replied, 'Your signet and your cord, and the staff that is in your hand.' So he gave them to her, and went in to her, and she conceived by him. Then she got up and went away, and taking off her veil she put on the garments of her widowhood.

When Judah sent the kid by his friend the Adullamite, to recover the pledge from the woman, he could not find her. He asked the townspeople, 'Where is the temple prostitute who was at Enaim by the wayside?' But they said, 'No prostitute has been here.' So he returned to Judah, and said, 'I have not found her; moreover the townspeople said, "No prostitute has been here."' Judah replied, 'Let her keep the things as her own, otherwise we will be laughed at; you see, I sent this kid, and you could not find her.'

About three months later Judah was told, 'Your daughter-in-law Tamar has played the whore; moreover she is pregnant as a result of whoredom.' And Judah said, 'Bring her out, and let her be burned.' As she was being brought out, she sent word to her father-in-law, 'It was the owner of these who made me pregnant.' And she said, 'Take note, please, whose these are, the signet and the cord and the staff.' Then Judah acknowledged them and said, 'She is more in the right than I, since I did not give her to my son Shelah.' And he did not lie with her again.

When the time of her delivery came, there were twins in her womb. While she was in labor, one put out a hand; and the midwife took and bound on his hand a crimson thread, saying, 'This one came out first.' But just then he drew back his hand, and out came his brother; and she said, 'What a breach you have made for yourself!' Therefore he was named Perez. Afterward his brother came out with the crimson thread on his hand; and he was named Zeerah.

(NRSV Genesis 38.1–30)

This is a story of female determination in a patriarchal culture, and it is also a story about a woman who breaches the incest taboo in order to guarantee her own security. In a male-dominated, patriarchal society, the plight of the single, childless female was precarious. The institution of Levirate marriage, by means of which the brother of a dead man took responsibility for his brother's widow and treated her as his own wife, was presumably introduced to offer some sort of protection to widows. In the case of Tamar, however, the system does not work. Onan, by *coitus interruptus*, makes sure she does not get pregnant, and it is pretty obvious that she is not going to be given to Shelah as his wife. So, like the daughters of Lot, she takes steps to protect her status and provide for her security by an act of incestuous prostitution. Interestingly again, the Bible tells us that from her two sons, Perez and Zerah, will come forth a long line of famous figures, including David, Solomon and Jesus of Nazareth. As with the story of Lot's daughters, the account of Tamar's seduction of her father-in-law is offered without comment or priestly hand-wringing, although some commentators see the nervous touch of a later editor in the assertion in verse twenty-six that Judah *did not lie with her again*. In both of these passages we are in touch with a strand of ancient biblical history for which sex as sex is not problematic, but only insofar as it is the occasion of or vehicle for purely human or dynastic struggles. These passages breathe the same uncontaminated air as the great heroic narratives in Homer, where it is the human situation itself that is problematic, not its sexual expression.

When we turn to the New Testament there is not much material to work on and none of it is systematically expounded. We look in on an emerging tradition, but there is little that would suggest the fateful turn it would take in later centuries. Much of what Paul says seems to be governed by his expectation of the imminent return of Christ and the end of the world. There was little point in developing a detailed ethic for human institutions and relationships that would soon be brought to an end. We probably have to exonerate Paul of the charge of misogyny, though some of the things he wrote are certainly capable of being interpreted in a sexist way. 'Stick it out where you are', was his message, 'because the time is shorter than you think'. There is even less about sex in the gospels and what we find there is capable of many interpretations. Unfortunately, since later generations of Christians loaded sexuality with terrifying significance, it is almost impossible to read the few New Testament texts there are on the subject except through the prism of their suspicion and hatred. If we doubt that claim, we should meditate on the following paradox. If we are to treat the Bible as a law book for all generations (an approach I would argue against anyway) why are we so keen to apply its alleged strictures against sexuality with such severity, while largely ignoring its much fiercer strictures against wealth and the damaging consequences of its pursuit, not only on our soul's health but on the lives of others? Why do we strain at the gnat of sexuality while swallowing camels laden with riches? Why are Church synods not riven with debate and threatened with schism over the Church's possession of riches? Why do rigorist clergy not break off communion with their bishops, because they live in palaces and are comfortable parts of the power structure, rather than because of their attitude to the intricacies of human sexual relationships? There clearly is a hidden agenda here, but there also seems to be a fairly straightforward account of where it came from.

According to Lawrence Osborne's book on sexual pessimism, *The Poisoned Embrace*, somewhere between the New Testament and the fourth century a strange anxiety entered Christianity's attitude to human sexuality. It came from the cult of Gnosticism, against which Catholic Christianity increasingly had to define itself. As is often the way in these titanic struggles, the Church absorbed as much as it rejected of its great opponent's ideas, very much the way New Labour, in its struggle for power, adopted many of the policies of its Conservative enemy. According to Hans Jonas, Gnosticism was the result of the fusion of three traditions: Hellenism, the margins of Judaism, and Persian Zoroastrianism. 'Hellenism provided the frame and much of the language. Judaism provided the mythological garb and the monotheism. And from the Persian root came Gnosticism's extreme dualism, its eschatological judgement and its pessimistic fatalism.'[9] Though very different in outlook, New Age spirituality provides us with a modern example of another eclectic religious movement that has had a profound effect on Christianity. In fact, we might argue that the fundamental optimism of New Age spirituality has provided an external corrective to the pessimism that was intruded into Christianity from dualistic Gnosticism. Certainly, books like Matthew Fox's *Original Blessing*[10] are self-conscious attempts to counter the ancient tradition in Christianity that is against the body and heavily emphasises human sinfulness at the expense of the doctrine of Creation as gift and blessing. Central to Gnostic teaching was a hatred of the body and its needs. A Gnostic text from the second century tells us:

> . . . he who has loved the body, which comes from the deceit of love, remains wandering in the darkness, suffering in his senses the things of death . . . it is because the source of the individual body is that abhorrent darkness from which the moist nature comes and from which the body is produced in the sensible world, and by which death is nourished . . . this bondage of corruption, this cloak of darkness, this living death, this sensate corpse, this tomb you carry around with you, this robber who lives in your house who by the things it loves hates you . . . Such is the hateful tunic with which you have clothed yourself; it holds you down in a stranglehold.[11]

Given this hysteria about the flesh, it is not surprising that the Gnostics persuaded themselves that they could be saved only by self-castration. Their excesses shocked even the most extreme Christian ascetics, but the Church's early cult of virginity and distrust of the body had its origin, not in Scripture, but in the hypnotic fever of the very heresy it tried to oppose. It is impossible to offer a full explanation today for the success of Gnostic sexual pessimism in infiltrating early Christianity. Osborne wonders if the terror of the venereal diseases which the Roman Empire spread through rapid urbanisation had something to do with it. We might also surmise that the emergence of a new and virulent strain of homophobia in the Church in our own time has something to do with the panic associated with AIDS and HIV. However we account for it, the Church's struggle with Gnosticism had a poisonous effect on the Christian attitude to human sexuality, though we should not ignore the gains as well as the losses. There is some evidence that the Church's pre-occupation with sex made the male of the human species more disciplined and gentle, so the very heresy that maligned the female also served to protect her in hard times. History is full of these consoling ironies. It also shows us how Christianity has always been profoundly influenced by external factors and ideas, some-times for good, sometimes for ill. That being the case, it seems appropriate to ask ourselves how we might develop a new ethic that will help us respond to the peculiar chal-lenges of our own time.

I have tried to show that our society, for perfectly valid reasons, is moving from a rules morality to a values morality, from a morality of command to a morality of consent. We no longer believe that any sexual act, as such, can be judged to be right or wrong except on moral grounds. You cannot define its moral nature from the sexual content alone. The morality of the act lies not in its sexuality, whatever it is, but on whether it causes harm to persons or their interests or violates their rights or causes injustice. We need to find a new, working definition of sexual harm for our own day, because the traditional approaches no longer help most people to deal with the complexity of modern relationships. Traditional religious systems had objective and easily understood definitions of harm. In the developed Christian tradition, as we have seen, sex was itself harmful and morally problematic; it was the means whereby sin entered human nature, so it had to be hedged about with protective mechanisms. Though it was an essential act for the procreation of children, the act itself was no longer straightforward, because desire or concupiscence had corrupted it. The early Christian interpretation of the Adam and Eve myth associated sex with sin, because it was through their original disobedience that sin had entered the world. The eternal innocence of the original couple had been succeeded by sexual desire and guilt; and their immortality had been replaced by death because, according to St Paul, 'the wages of sin is death' (Romans 6.23). We have already looked at some of the psychological consequences of this attitude to sex. It built into early Christian consciousness an association between sex, guilt and death that led to the heroically ascetic utopianism of some of the early Christian Fathers. It was imagined that, if virginity became universal, death itself might be defeated and the curse of Adam overturned. Thus was born the sexual problematic in Christianity. Women, by the pains of childbirth, would continue the race and at the same time partially purge the guilt of their sexuality, which was the cause of all our woe in the first place. This was the beginning of a complicated nexus that rendered sex itself intrinsically sinful, women as the lure to that sin, and their subjection the consequence. As long as women were tied to the cycle of childbirth and economic dependence on men, the complicated dynamic of the ancient sexual taboo still worked. There has been a revolution in our time that has rendered the Christian sexual taboo as obsolete as the Polynesian taboo against men and women eating with each other, though we do not yet quite know what to put in its place.

The main cause of the revolution has been the feminist revolt against the traditional subjection or subordination of women. And much of that revolt has been against the reproductive determinism that fixed the lives of women around childbearing and family management. Birth control methods have given women reproductive freedom for the first time in history: they can, if they choose, be in charge of their own reproductive destiny. Related to that is an increasing determination to achieve economic independence. Dependence on men of the sort that trapped generations of their forebears is not something most women are prepared to tolerate today. To many women, Christianity with its attitude to human sexuality is no longer a relevant force. Christianity has had too much to do with men who spend a lot of time justifying the exclusion of women. It does not seem to answer women's needs, because it inculcates a feel-bad factor and women spend enough time struggling with low self-esteem. Women's spiritual needs are not best met by institutions that are essentially instruments of hierarchy and guilt. While Christianity claims to be about relationships, it appears to many women to be a one-sided dialogue for which the script has already been written. And, while many women today may experience considerable sexual confusion, they are quite certain that traditional Christian norms no longer provide them with an appropriate language in which to describe their own sexual needs and aspirations.

It is here that the most surprising and radical reversal of the traditional Christian sexual ethic has taken place. There was always a double-standard in traditional attitudes to sex. Men were the pursuers, women the pursued. Men were expected to be sexually adventurous and sow their wild oats; women were expected to keep themselves for their husbands. Men were the initiators; women the passive recipients of their (often unwanted) attentions. Today, especially in youth culture, that double-standard has been completely obliterated. Youth culture is not unaware of sexual love and its implied commitments, but it has a tolerant attitude to what it calls *shagging*. In one significant section of youth culture, many young people shag or have sexual intercourse with each other whenever they feel like it, the way they have a cup of coffee or a hamburger. Sex is an appetite to be satisfied, with no necessary connection to any kind of relationship. It is part of a good night out, like drugs and drink. Shagging is about sexual sensation, and women go for it with the same determination as men. Here is a statement that defines the attitude of some of the young woman to today's sex culture. It is spoken by a male of the species who has just caught on to something surprising:

Yo, listen up: they've figured the game. A 90s woman is out hawking sex just like you. You ain't playing her no more. She's playing you. She will dump you just like a dude will. She will fuck you and not call back. She will mess with your mind. She'll tell you straight up, 'I got what I want, now get out of my bed.' Before the 90s, women were on a feral hunt. They were getting dogged and we programmed them to get dogged. We said, 'You ain't got nothing for me.' Now they say, 'OK motherfucker, cool. Check this out: we ain't dealing with no more o' your shit.' A 90s woman ain't having it. She watched her momma go through hell with her pops, and she ain't having it. She doesn't need you. She says, 'We're in love. Let's kick it until we ain't in love, and then I'm out of here.' So now you're in for a real ride, because only one of y'all is wearing the pants and it may not be you.[12]

It would not be true to say that the young people who adopt this approach to shagging are necessarily without any ethic of sexuality. They separate shagging from sexual love. Shagging is purely functional, pleasurable in its own right, done for its own sake. If it leads to sexual love and the development of a steady relationship a different code comes in to play. The relationship, while it lasts, has to be sexually exclusive or honest about other sexual encounters. The emotional connection alters the ethical dynamic in a subtle way. An emotional relationship creates a bond that opens each person in the couple to the possibility of injury or harm as a result of the conduct of the other. The implicit ethic identifies that potential harm as the focus of the moral concern. Infidelity hurts, causes damage, therefore it is wrong. In shagging there is no bond that can be broken, unless the person out shagging is also in a sexually exclusive relationship. Sexual love and its discipline of faithfulness, while the relationship endures, is a contemporary version of the traditional ethic of marriage. It indicates the continuing strength of the principle of monogamy (even though it is now serial monogamy) as an institution that has an implicit moral structure based on the importance of protecting ourselves from the damage and harm our sexual and emotional needs can do to one another. Traditional supporters of marriage may see this new ethic as a severely attenuated version of the old one, but it does bear witness to the continuity of the moral principle that informed the sexual aspect of marriage. It is clearly based on the principle that sexual commitment, however temporary, creates the possibility of violation and harm unless the disciplines of exclusivity are followed by both partners. A clear sexual ethic is implicitly and explicitly operating in the apparently chaotic culture of youth sexuality.

What about the morality of shagging? Does the principle of harm operate here as well? Traditionalists would claim that to treat something as sacred as sexuality in such a trivial way is intrinsically harmful and demeaning and should, therefore, be avoided. Obviously, if we believe that the act of sexual intercourse creates an ontological or spiritual bond, as well as an immediately physical one, then any casual use of sexuality will be abominated. Intact religious communities will teach various versions of the ontological argument against casual sex, but it is difficult to demonstrate its validity to those who do not accept the premises on which the prohibition is based. They would argue that sex between freely consenting adults, with no other binding commitments, harms no one in any obviously verifiable way. If we listen to John Harris's test of moral verifiability this might become clearer: 'For a moral judgement to be respectable it must have something to say about just why a supposed wrong action is wrongful. If it fails to meet this test it is a preference and not a moral judgement at all.'[13] We may find the shagging culture aesthetically displeasing, like teenage drinking and general rebelliousness; but unless we believe that sexual intercourse is always wrong, except in carefully prescribed circumstances, we cannot simply dismiss shagging as immoral behaviour. We may want to argue against it for perfectly good reasons; we may want to cite it as an example of purely instinctive behaviour ungoverned by the specifically human attributes of reason and consciousness. But we ought to be careful about dismissing it as immoral behaviour that harms others or does them an injury or causes injustice. Young people have an arguable need to overdo things that are all right in themselves, such as drinking and making a noise and general exuberance. In their sexual experimentation they are likely to overdo things in the same way. Young people always push against the norms that operate in their communities, always tend towards excess and tastelessness. We are more likely to win their consent to responsible conduct if we do not crank the moral claim beyond the level of arguability. There is a definite need for the recovery of a sense of balance in human sexuality, so that we do not constantly swing between the extremes of abnegation and over-indulgence. And any guidelines we adopt will have to be applicable to gay and lesbian people as well as to heterosexual people. They are an inalienable part of the human community, and should be accorded the same privileges and be expected to fulfil the same responsibilities as everyone else.

CHAPTER THREE

Was the Trojan Horse Gay?

Napier University in Edinburgh has a widely scattered series of campuses, but its main administration block is in a giant Italian villa a couple of miles south of Princes Street. The building was opened in 1880 as the Craiglockhart Hydropathic Institution. It occupies a magnificent site and its central tower commands one of the best views in Scotland, looking away over the Firth of Forth to the distant mountains of Perthshire. The original facilities had included Turkish and swimming baths, and 'ladies' and gentlemen's special bath-rooms, with all the varieties of hot and cold plunge, vapour, spray, needle, douche and electrical baths, with special galvanic apparatus'. In spite of these impressive amenities the place had never prospered and in 1916 it was taken over by the Army for officers suffering from shell-shock. If it had not existed, some of the best poetry in the English language might never have been. written.

In July 1917 an army officer who was already a well-known poet, Siegfried Sassoon, published 'A Soldier's Declaration', in which he made an act of wilful defiance of military authority, because he believed that the war was being deliberately prolonged by those who had the power to end it. Afraid that his friend would be court-martialled, Robert Graves fixed it with the Army for Sassoon to be sent to Craiglockhart War Hospital where he was treated by the remarkable army psychologist W.H.R. Rivers. Though he never retracted his statement, Sassoon went back to active service in France, because he felt that his work was now to tell the world through his poetry what the war was really like. The whole episode was beautifully fictionalised in Pat Barker's novel, *Regeneration*,[1] and was later made into a fine movie, to which I shall return in a minute. Sassoon in 1917 was already a mature poet with an authentic voice. The same could hardly be said for Wilfrid Owen, whom he met at Craiglockhart that summer.

Owen was born in 1893 in Shropshire, where his father was a railway worker. He had always longed to go to university and become an educated man, but Shrewsbury Technical College was all his family could afford and he was always a bit self-conscious about his modest background and provincial accent. Beneath the diffidence, however, there was a formidable human being who emerged to be the greatest of Britain's World War I poets. After a period assisting in a country parish (he contemplated ordination at one time), he left in 1913 to teach English in Bordeaux and returned in 1915 to join the army. He was commissioned in the Manchester Regiment in 1916 and on 30 December was sent out to the base camp at Etaples. In March 1917, after days under fire, he fell asleep on a railway embankment, somewhere near Savy Wood, and was blown into the air by a shell, a near-miss that left him helpless, lying close to the dismembered remains of another officer. When he got back to camp, people noticed that he was in shock. Inevitably, the commanding officer called his courage into question. Fortunately, the doctor diagnosed 'neurasthenia' and it was decided that the best place for him would be Craiglockhart War Hospital in Edinburgh. He arrived there in June 1917.

Owen had experimented with verse from an early age, and had read widely, but in 1917 his work was still self-consciously poetic when he took it shyly along the corridor at Craiglockhart to Sassoon. Sassoon, whom he fell for instantly, taught him that poetry was about reality and helped him to see that it was the war he must deal with. Sassoon's friendship and advice released Owen's genius, and the final year of his life gave us the poetry that we remember today. In one of his notebooks Owen scribbled a preface to the poems that were not to be published till four years after his death in 1920:

> Above all, I am not concerned with Poetry.
> My subject is War, and the Pity of War.
> The poetry is in the Pity.[2]

The film *Regeneration* is based on Pat Barker's fiction about this episode. The irony of the regime at Craiglockhart, brought out very well in the movie, is that the deeply understanding and sympathetic Doctor Rivers, who understood the horror these men had gone through, cured his patients in order to send them back to the front. Though Sassoon and Owen had lost belief in the war, they went back to it willingly, Owen to the front, where he was killed a week before the war ended, shepherding his men through an artillery barrage on the Sambre Canal in November 1918. It is impossible to read his poems, which are filled with contempt for those who drove the war on and love and compassion for the soldiers who were its victims, without feeling an angry love rise in you. The film provokes a similar anger and love, and I watched it with deep emotion. Most of the anger I felt was against the folly of the ruling ascendancy who sent all those brave young men 'to die as cattle', in Owen's own phrase. But that was only part of my anger; the other part had a different root.

These two men, both extraordinarily brave, both poets who enriched our literature, and one of whom, Owen, was a great poet whose work will endure, were gay, though theirs was a love that dared not speak its name at that time. Had the establishment that exploited them and sent them to the trenches found out about their true nature they would have hounded them to another sort of death. Sassoon, the warrior scholar, gave Owen more than the freedom to be a great poet; he also gave him the courage to accept his own nature, and these two freedoms were almost certainly related. By saying no to the war and yes to himself, Owen's genius was liberated. Sassoon introduced him to his London friends, who included Robert Ross, the great Wildean loyalist, and Osbert Sitwell. Through them he got to know Charles Scott-Moncrieff, who fell in love with him, and who was to make use of Owen's experiments with assonance in his great translation of Proust.

After his release from Craiglockhart, Owen trained at Scarborough and Ripon, but his return to duty was punctuated by visits to London to see his new friends, all of whom seem to have recognised his genius as a poet almost immediately. He had found love, and through that love he had found his work: War, and the Pity of War. Owen's tender, yet angry, love for his men surges through his poetry. It was why he went back to the front a determined soldier. Early in October he won the Military Cross on the Hindenburg Line, even though he hated the war and no longer found any virtue in it. Like E.M. Forster, another gay man of genius, his loyalties now were to his friends, not to the great establishments that rob us of our humanity as they seduce us with the blandishments of their approval. Owen died for his friends, and I find in his death and in the great poetry that came before it an ikon, a representational symbol, of the place of gay and lesbian people in our culture, and especially in the culture of the Church. In this chapter I want to address the subject of the status of gay men and lesbian women in Christianity; and I want to retain that edge of emotion about this subject that the film *Regeneration* generated in me, because we are confronting a culture, not only of injustice, but of ingratitude for the contribution that gay and lesbian people have made to the life of the Church down the centuries.

I have given the chapter a rather dramatic title, because many commentators allege that the issue of human sexuality is creating a new fault line in Christianity along which new divisions could emerge. It is alleged that living with the contradictions of gay and lesbian sexuality will be one challenge too many for even the most tolerant and liberal of churches, and their unity will finally disintegrate like Troy. I am not a fortune-teller, so I cannot say whether that pessimistic prediction will come true. If Christians do come apart over this issue, however, it will be because of disagreements over theology and philosophy, not because of sex. The sexuality debate is a symptom or expression of a deeper, more substantive conflict about truth and the ways we apprehend it. So if the Christian Church does break up, it will be because of profound, not superficial matters; it will be because of issues far more important than sexuality. That is why I want to summarise and draw conclusions from my argument so far, before focusing on this substantive conflict about truth, particularly in relation to scripture, and then returning to the gay and lesbian issue as an example of the way in which an underlying philosophical conflict expresses itself.

I have taken up a point of view in this book about the nature and role of morality. I have claimed that morality is a human construct; it is something that we ourselves have created. This may seem too obvious to be disputed, until we remember that many of our moral traditions claim to be the mind and command of God. Bringing God into the moral debate is problematic, however, no matter how we respond. If we think of God as the dictator of our moral systems, we run into difficulties when we confront their dynamic and changeful nature. We have already observed the difficulty believers encounter when they conclude that a given commandment or custom is one that their reason can no longer accept. The example I have used is the role and status of women and their freedom to share with men privileges and opportunities from which they were historically excluded by divine command. If there is no longer any acceptable reason why women should be excluded from a particular human role, other than the commandment of God, then we have created a crisis for our understanding of God. This is why many conservative interpreters of scripture are in a state of confusion over the role of women in the Church. According to the most straightforward reading of some of the things Saint Paul says, women should not hold positions of leadership over men, because man is the head of woman. This places us in a dilemma today. We either have to deny the evidence of history and our own experience, which shows that women are just as likely to be good leaders as men, or we deny the infallibility of Paul. The sane and obvious thing to do is to say that Paul got it wrong or, more appropriately, that what might have been right for Paul's day is wrong for ours. If we take that sane and rational approach, however, we relativise and contextualise the way we use God and the claims we have historically made on behalf of God. We are, as it were, putting the word 'God' into quotation marks when we use it in moral discourse. We may claim, for instance, that it is the way we emphasise the seriousness of a particular moral tradition, but we dare not treat it as the last word on the subject, because last words are usually overtaken by events, even in religion.

This is not the same thing as saying that none of the moral traditions for which we claim divine sanction has permanent authority over us. Some ancient moral traditions still have self-evidencing authority, but it is their ethical appropriateness that gives them authority, not their divine warrant. 'Thou shalt do no murder' is a moral imperative in any civilised society, accepted by unbelievers and believers alike, because of its obviousness. In other words, we hold the principle on moral, not theological, grounds. We justify it by reference to the way in which violating it would cause harm to persons or their interests or violate their rights or cause injustice. The argument from divine sanction, by itself, does none of these things. We obey the command-ment against killing because murder obviously violates the important moral principle that we should not harm persons, not because it is a divine command. This is why I quoted John Harris in the last chapter as saying that, 'For a moral judgement to be respectable it must have something to say about just why a supposed wrong action is wrongful. If it fails to meet this test it is a preference and not a moral judgement at all.'³ To meet this test, it is clearly not enough to quote the authority of God.

Morality is something we construct in response to the tension created by nature or the life-force and the sense of personal responsibility that human consciousness creates. All of this is seen with particular clarity in the area of sexuality, where the life-force or pressure of the species is indifferent to our own personal contentment and creates an acute personal tension within us. Sexual morality is our attempt to order and contain that tension. But we have already seen how many of these moral constructions are arbitrary and revisable. This is why it is important to understand them from within their original contexts, as far as we are able to do so. There is an inescapable tendency to solidify our experiments into traditions, to establish them as normative, so that they guarantee our automatic consent. As we have seen, traditions work as long as they operate in this unconscious way; they fail when we begin to question them and start withdrawing our consent from them. This begins to happen when the tradition is no longer in living touch with the original context that gave it power and plausibility.

God's role is problematic, whichever way we jump. We have already seen that the solution that treats the whole tradition as an unchanging divine imperative is likely to be sunk in the flow of change that characterises human experience, bringing God into contempt with those who, for highly moral reasons, can no longer accept a particular element of the tradition. This is why many of the debates among religious believers end up sounding like the war in *Gulliver's Travels* between those who insisted that a boiled egg should only be opened at the big end and those who insisted on the sharp end. All that is left is the taboo or prohibition, long since uncoupled from the context in which it originally made some kind of sense. The main difficulty for religious traditions is the way they associate God exclusively with their opinions. We can argue against an obvious human injustice, we can demonstrate the absurdity of a particular type of intolerance, we can poke fun at bigotry and hatred, but how can we argue against God? This is the problem that religions have faced at every stage of history. If they are persuaded that the human arrangements that characterise a particular phase of human development and understanding are the final will and commandment of God, how can they ever make appropriate changes to their life? Many passionately honest people today believe that traditional religions have shown themselves to be incapable of making these liberating changes, so they have abandoned them completely as primitive superstitions incapable of development. This is why many feminists have left the Church. They see it as incurably patriarchal and oppressive towards women in both its theology and its structures; they believe that the only adult thing for women to do is to leave it and find their own maturity in freedom, the way people sometimes have to walk away from abusive and oppressive parents if they are ever to grow up. The thing that has most frustrated feminists who campaigned for equality in the Church was not that the men in charge said honestly that they did not want to share power with women, or that they liked all the male language about God in the bible because it flattered their own sense of gender superiority – there would be a certain kind of refreshing honesty in that, and the laughter it provoked might itself be cleansing and transforming. But that's not what they said. They said, 'We ourselves have no prejudices against women; indeed, if it were up to us we would alter things to accommodate their obvious frustrations; unfortunately, God has different ideas. He has fixed these things for ever, and who are we to fight against God?' It is the identification of God with transient social attitudes that is religion's greatest strength and its greatest weakness. It is this supreme confidence that gives religion its power, but at the price of building into it the cause of its own destruction.

Nevertheless, an important subtlety must be observed here. Human freedom of choice, even if the choice is irrational, is one of our important values, provided it does not clash with other, even more important values. People have the right to opt for what is called an intact moral community, if they want to. An intact moral community is a body, such as a religious group, that chooses to maintain an existing tradition in its entirety, in spite of the critical erosions of time and change upon it. Choosing to submit to an intact moral system is one way of avoiding the pain and expenditure of time that moral dilemmas place us in. We rarely reach final, universally compelling conclusions in moral debate, but we do have to make decisions for our own lives and the lives of others. The root meaning of the word 'decide' suggests the activity of cutting through, rather than painstakingly unravelling, a tangled knot. One way of dealing with moral complexities is to opt into a system and let it decide for us. This does not deliver us completely from intellectual argument, however, because we will continue to live in a larger culture that embraces a number of other moral approaches, but our act of submission to a particular system removes moral uncertainty from our lives by transferring it to an external authority whose judgements we obey. In other words, opting into an intact moral community will not deliver us from the pains of disagreement with others, though it may, as a decision in intellectual economy, release us from personal doubt. There may be friction with other intact moral communities that operate from different premises, and there will certainly be conflict with groups that maintain an open approach to disputed questions.

This book is not about the existence of God and the intellectual difficulties that certain ways of holding faith create for believers, but if we hold that there is a reality to which our word 'God' refers, which is more than the sum of our aspirations and longings, we are not thereby freed from the need to make choices in the kind of world we live in. Whatever choices we make, even choices that claim to be prompted by God, we shall remain inescapably fixed on the human side of these dilemmas. We can only know the divine mystery and the life it commends from within our own human experience, because no other experience is available to us. There is no Archimedean point outside our own experience from which we can survey the issue and pronounce upon it. We always see through the dark glass of our humanity, even when we are looking at God. A legitimate way of arguing, therefore, would be that if there is a reality which we think of as the divine mystery it could be expressing itself through the plural, striving and incomplete nature of the universe itself. Whether we think of the universe as being in God or God as being in the universe, we have to acknowledge that God is experienced in the struggle of life and not in some magical rescue from it. The only other coherent approach that retains belief in God is the kind of dualism that pits the creation against God, and this causes more problems than it solves and usually creates contempt for the created order. Dualistic systems, as we saw in the last chapter, always end by creating a gulf between God and nature that can only be bridged by some mediating system, knowledge of which becomes the prerequisite of an official caste or priesthood.

The vice of all official systems is that the power relation, the need to control or be in charge of the exploration, takes over and inhibits our ability to go on asking questions and struggling with truth. We have already noticed the ancient and important distinction between the priestly and prophetic poles in religion. The tension between the two types is expressed, though never resolved, in the Bible. It is true that the priestly, controlling type of consciousness retrojected into scripture a dominant editorial overview, but the prophetic voice was never silenced, the voice of the critic and satirist, the voice we hear in Jesus. All official, priestly systems, whether political or religious, operate in the same way. Literary fabrication becomes necessary, what Plato would have called the necessary lie, so sacred books are discovered and imposed with great solemnity upon the people. The evils that have befallen the nation or the sacred community, it is claimed, were the result of estrangement from the sacred text which has now been miraculously recovered and must be severely imposed by the priestly elite, whether it is a political cadre or a caste of sacred officials. Priesthoods, sacred or secular, all operate through the concept of sin or fault. Priests create a place of power for themselves by getting into position between nature and God, or humanity and political ideology. They become the mediators of value and truth, and disobedience of their law acquires the name 'sin'. Conveniently, the means of becoming reconciled, whether with God or the Party, operates in a way that establishes the priest more thoroughly in the mediating role, the role of fixer or broker: the priest alone redeems. This was one of the assumptions that Jesus, speaking from within the prophetic tradition, challenged by his claim that the kingdom of God, in Dominic Crossan's phrase, was 'brokerless'; it required no mediator, so that people did not have to be issued passports by the priesthood to achieve access to God. Jesus said that he had come to remit sin, and his most radical parables are all about a divine forgiveness that precedes human repentance. Nietzsche, who revered Christ but hated Christianity, gives us an echo of this prophetic voice in scripture that is challenged but never defeated by the priestly megaphone. He wrote:

From a psychological point of view, 'sins' are indispensable in any society organised by priests: they are the actual levers of power, the priest lives on sins, he needs 'the commission of sins'. . . . Supreme law: 'God forgives him who repents' – in plain language: who subjects himself to the priest.[4]

By *sin* priests usually mean the private struggles of individuals, rarely the oppression of systems, and hardly ever the systems *they* serve. All priesthoods or official systems are in constant danger of living parasitically on the anguish we experience in searching for honest ways to live in a world of competing claims. They count upon our weariness, our longing to be rescued from struggle and uncertainty in one bound. We can have compassion for the human need to be rescued from the burden of freedom in this way; we can even see the stabilising effect that some total systems have had upon human anarchy; but we also have to admit that they can be an abdication of human strength and freedom, a handing over of these precious gifts to the powerful, a withdrawal from the struggle. For personal reasons, we may choose one of these absolute solutions, the way people with spare capital sometimes hand it over to investment companies to manage for them. That can be a sensible way to manage our intellectual economy. It will give us the security of knowing that we have a large and prudent tradition behind us. What we cannot do, however, is claim that this is the only way to practise in the market of ideas. If God is ultimate reality, then all truth must be contained in that reality, so all struggle with truth is engagement with God, even if it appears to be a rejection of the claims tradition makes about God. The saying, *If you meet the Buddha on the road, kill him,* is a warning against all traditions that claim to have an exclusive patent on the mind of God. Just as we are increasingly recognising the rich plurality of human cultures and traditions, even contradictory ones, so must we recognise the height and depth and variety of the human experience of God. This means that we can go on exploring the mystery of God, while retaining an appropriate, if critical, awareness of the traditions that have come down to us. We will recognise the important value of continuity, but we will also acknowledge the danger of human laziness and the seductive effect of powerful interests upon the human longing for painless stability.

This means that it is important to go on thinking about our approach to what is called 'revelation', especially in its written form. The concept of revelation as a direct or unmediated word from God transmitted through human agents to the printed page has been critically eroded by the knowledge we now have of the history of the formation of ancient texts. The unsettling effect of this cumulative process of erosion gives a specious respectability to those who call for 'an all or nothing' approach to the Bible. Once you start picking and choosing, it is claimed, the whole thing unravels. There is considerable intellectual dishonesty in this approach, however, because it refuses to acknowledge that even avowed traditionalists have a hierarchy of value in their interpretation of scripture. I pointed out in the last chapter the significant disparity in the way Christians have interpreted the many strictures on money and possessions in the New Testament, compared with their approach to the paucity of texts on the subject of human sexuality. The debate on the ordination of women has already caused a massive reconsideration of Christian attitudes to the authority of particular texts. We need to take the process further and find the courage to rethink our attitude to the authority of scripture as a whole and how we should use it today. As we do this, however, we shall have to acknowledge that there will always be an asymmetry between the personal and official approaches to this matter, not unlike the distinction between the prophetic and the priestly approaches to the mystery of God and the nature of the world. The Church as a priestly edifice will always contend for the traditional understanding of scriptural authority, because it bolsters its own claim to be the official mediator between the divine and the human. The prophetic approach, on the other hand, will have more regard for the truth of experience than for official dogma or institutional stability, and will have a particular suspicion of texts that are used as excuses for punishing or devaluing people. The real moral issue here ought to be, not the meaning of the texts themselves, but the appalling way they have been used as a justification for the persecution and punishment of our fellow human beings.

Amnesty International's report, *Breaking the Silence*, contains a horrifying catalogue of human rights violations against people, based on their sexual orientation. The report presents dozens of carefully documented cases from countries all over the world. It shows us that, half a century after Hitler's extermination policy for gays and other social deviants blackened the skies of Europe with smoke from the gas ovens, homophobia is still alive and violently kicking, and much of it is motivated by religious zeal, as was powerfully demonstrated by the Lambeth Conference of 1998. This ten-yearly meeting of Anglican bishops from all over the world, in re-affirming Christianity's traditional rejection of same-sex relationships, evinced a degree of hatred of homosexuals that many observers found frightening, causing one of the bishops present to liken it to a Nuremburg rally. The saddest aspect of a very depressing event was the way speaker after speaker quoted the Bible as though it was the final word on a complex subject, so that no further thinking needed to be done.

One of the paradoxes of scripture is the presence within it of a prophetic, self-contradictory tradition that calls us to overthrow systems that claim to mediate the God who needs no mediator. The distinguished Old Testament scholar Walter Brueggemann says that the Torah corrects the Torah. This is why we should not shirk the task of rethinking the authority of the Bible over our lives, allowing the living scripture of our own experience to challenge the dead letter of the written law. We have always done this with written scripture, though rarely with complete candour. We have always found ways to get round the obvious meaning of a text when it no longer conforms to our own understanding of value and truth. And, contrary to what traditionalists often say, this is not because we want to avoid hard sayings that cause us discomfort. We are all experts at pointing out the importance of texts that bring pain to others, while carefully avoiding the ones that challenge our own comforts. The rich always find it easy to call upon the poor to make sacrifices they would never dream of making themselves. Heterosexuals, especially Christian heterosexuals, are expert at calling upon homosexuals to deny themselves consolations they themselves could not live without. We are all inescapably caught in a web of complicity here, so we should be careful about rushing to judgement on our troubled neighbours. The heart of the message of Jesus was a challenge to the powerful to acknowledge their complicity in the fact of human misery. Only the destitute were innocent, he told them; only the wretched were guiltless; only those who had no bread had no fault. And in today's debate about human sexuality he would probably say that only the gay are without hypocrisy.

WAS THE TROJAN HORSE GAY?

Paradoxically, it is scripture itself that calls us to overturn scripture; it is the witness of the living word of Jesus that challenges us to follow the logic that scripture was made for humanity and not humanity for scripture. We should not, therefore, have to torture scripture into self-contradictory positions, when it no longer conforms to our experience of truth and value. It is much more honest to abandon it, acknowledging that it witnesses to an earlier, no longer appropriate, attitude to human relationships. We have done this over its attitude to slavery; we have done it over its attitude to usury or the taking of interest, the very basis of the modern global market economy; we seem unable to make this liberating change in our attitude to human sexuality, because of the moral virus that invaded the Christian bloodstream during its encounter with Gnosticism. It cannot be the texts that cause the problem, because we are adept at eluding the force of texts we reject in other contexts. But how are we to think about the texts themselves; why have such claims been made on their behalf?

We are involved in an inescapable circularity here. Christians say the Bible is inspired, because the Bible itself tells them so, but what do we mean by the claim? We use the term in secular ways, so we might find a clue there. We talk about the *canon* of scripture and the word suggests measurement or comparison. These books have a certain definitive quality about them compared with lesser works, we say. And we apply the same criterion to secular literature. Scholars talk about the Western literary canon, for instance. Individuals may disagree about the right of particular authors to a place in the canon, but they would agree that there is a continuum of excellence, and it is an interesting and amusing game to place the names of dead, white, mainly male writers on the list. We would probably all agree that writing covers a wide spectrum of value, just like food. Some writing is the equivalent of junk-food, quick and stimulating, but of no enduring value to us; other writing has the ability to go on challenging and delighting generations. We can be fairly certain that, a century from now, people will still be reading and performing Shakespeare, whereas the latest thriller on the best seller list will be unremembered. Shakespeare is in the canon, today's best sellers probably never will be. The same is true of music, probably the highest of the human arts. The discerning recognise the intrinsic quality of good art, they are compelled by its self-evidencing greatness. There is a canon of Western philosophy, as well, even though it has been described as nothing but a footnote to Plato. The Bible is one of these canons in its own right. In fact, it is a whole library, containing books of widely differing quality. Stuart Blanch captured its quality very well in a single paragraph.

Imagine 'Gibbon's Decline and Fall of the Roman Empire, the collected poems of T.S. Eliot, the Textus Roffensis, Hamlet, Robinson's Honest to God, The Canterbury Tales, Holinshed's Chronicles, the Cathedral Statutes of Rochester, Hymns Ancient and Modern (Revised), Bonhoeffer's Letters and Papers from Prison, Hammersjkold's Markings, The Thoughts of Chairman Mao, Pilgrim's Progress, the Sixteen Satires of Juvenal and the Book of Kells' deprived of indications of date and authorship, all printed in the same format and bound together as a single volume; the analogy suggests that it is natural that the library comprising the Jewish and Christian Scriptures manifests such diversity of viewpoint.[5]

The Bible is the record of a particular set of experiences of the human encounter with the meaning of God. As Stuart Blanch's words suggest, it varies enormously within itself.

There are obvious differences of quality between, say, the official, priestly version of Old Testament history in the Book of Chronicles and the white-hot prophecies of Jeremiah or the three writers in the book of Isaiah. There is an equally obvious disparity in the New Testament between, say, the Letters of James and II Peter, and Paul's magnificent Letter to the Romans. It is always the same test that is applied. We do not revere the books because of their official status, but because of their intrinsic value. In fact, the books that claim too much for themselves, the official texts, are transparent in their special pleading, like all propaganda, and leave us cold or make us angry; while the great prophecies of Isaiah or the parables of Jesus, even if we cannot fully understand them, challenge and exalt us still. In all of this we are already doing the wise and obvious thing; we are recognising that inspired material, like good wine, needs no 'bush' or advertisement for itself, no official authorisation requiring our consent. It compels our assent by its own quality, and our judgement of that quality is a crucial part of the revelatory process. What we bring to scripture, therefore, is as important as what we get from it. We are inescapably led to the acknowledgement of a canon within a canon in our use of the Bible, as in our use of all great literature and art; but we have to go further. Is any of it to be taken as positive law and, if so, by what principle of discernment?

Shakespeare usually exalts and stimulates me, but I do not believe that Polonius's speech to Laertes in *Hamlet* has legal authority over me, though much of it is sound advice. Why should I offer Saint Paul a different treatment? We have already seen how we dealt with Paul over the place of women in the Church. Common sense prevailed over any claim that Paul's strictures had permanent authority for us.

They were a photograph of the customs of his day, but we persuaded ourselves that they were no longer normative for our time. The same has to be said of the few things that Paul said about same-sex relations in the Letter to the Romans in chapter one. 'They have exchanged the truth of God for a lie, and have offered reverence and worship to created things instead of to the Creator. Blessed is he for ever, Amen. As a result God has given them up to shameful passions. Among them women have exchanged natural intercourse for unnatural, and men too, giving up natural relations with women, burn with lust for one another; males behave indecently with males, and are paid in their own persons the fitting wage of such perversion.' We can try to torture a liberal interpretation out of that text by claiming that Paul did not understand same-sex relations in the way we now do, so his strictures, which seem to be based on fear of idol worship of some sort, cannot apply to our time. The really honest way for us to deal with the question is to ask: even if Paul would have opposed what we mean by same-sex relations, why should his opposition be normative for us today? In other parts of Pauline theology we make choices. We might find his metaphors for explaining the power of Christ's death suggestive, and his doctrine of God's justifying grace liberating; we are no longer likely to make much of his expectation of the imminent return of Jesus, and some of us find his certainty that all rulers get their authority from God dangerous as well as unconvincing. Sensibly, we make choices here, we take what still has authority for us, because of its self-evidencing power, and reject the rest. In fact, we no longer treat an injunction from scripture as having moral authority over us simply because it is in scripture. It has to have moral force independent of its scriptural context. We judge scripture by our own best moral standards, not the other way round. We now do this in most areas except the area of sexual behaviour. We must find the honesty and courage to apply this criterion of authenticity to the tangled area of human sexuality.

One of the fascinating things about the campaign for equal human rights for gay and lesbian people is that most of the energy for it, and most of the progress it has achieved, has been in society at large, rather than within the Christian Church. This should not surprise us, because the impetus for social reform usually happens in this way, with the Church right at the back of the procession. It is significant that, the day after the vote in the House of Commons to lower the age of consent for gay sex to 16, the *Guardian* newspaper wrote that homosexuality had just curled up and died as a political issue in Britain. The piece ended with these words: 'This topic has expired. You might as well try to repeal legislation on child chimney sweeps.' That is certainly true as far as the political order goes. In the Christian Church it will take a bit longer. That is why some of us are still trying to push the Trojan Horse through the gates.

CHAPTER FOUR

What is Your Poison?

Morality is more an art than a science and it calls for a certain versatility from us, that ability to improvise and respond to actual circumstances which I mentioned in chapter 1. We have already noticed that when we start thinking about value systems we involve ourselves in conflicts that appear to have no simple solution. Human nature is so varied, and the things we consider important are so different, that it is often impossible to do more than describe the values that are in conflict and let people make their own choices. Choice itself, as we have also seen, is something that is rarely straightforward; it is usually influenced by factors over which we have little control, some of which are particular to our own history, and some of which are the result of general conditions in the human environment. These factors have always added complexity to the moral debate, but there can be little doubt that our confusions today are particularly acute. This is not because we are less interested in or committed to the moral life than we used to be, which is what is often alleged by particular interest groups. It is because of the accelerating pace of change in society, so that many of the institutions or traditions that previously formed and policed our values have themselves been undermined, if not actually destroyed, by the sheer momentum of history. In the past, value systems were carried and inculcated by the confident existence of traditional structures and institutions, such as family, Church, school, monarchy, as well as the unspoken set of attitudes that underlined them. The word to describe this complex value-bearing system is tradition. A tradition is the way we do things; it is handed on from generation to generation; and by definition it has been accepted and internalised, not as one possible approach among many others, but as *the* way in which things have to be done if chaos and confusion are to be avoided. We can all think of examples of this phenomenon, many of them giving rise to the kind of farcical rigidity or misunderstanding that is the staple of human comedy and tragedy, such as the hapless stranger in church who was rudely ejected from her pew by the irate regular who 'always sits there', or the avoidable naval disaster caused by a short-sighted admiral who ordered two columns of battleships to reverse direction by turning inwards, with predictable consequences already obvious to the junior officers present, who were not prepared to challenge an order which they knew would lead to great loss of life, because it was not their place to challenge authority.

We describe our society as post-traditional, because we no longer offer unquestioning obedience to any institution or set of attitudes and approaches simply because it has been around for a long time. Set down on paper like that, the claim seems to be straightforward and unarguable, but it has had a revolutionary impact on the way we live and the way we think about ourselves. There can be little argument about the agent that has caused this change: it is the dominance of the global market economy and the social and cultural movements that have accompanied its ascendance. The normal condition of modern capitalism is permanent and dynamic disorder, the opposite of the traditional equilibrium or steady state that we often look wistfully back at. One of the paradoxes of the present situation is that in Britain it was a conservative administration that created the conditions that led to the triumph of capitalism over traditional conservative values. In the 1980s the market and its relationship to the state were radically restructured by the removal of traditional restraints upon capital. The effect of this revolution has been amplified and universalised by modern information technology, which allows an increasing number of transactions to take place globally. This unfettering of the market has been paralleled by a number of cultural and social movements that questioned traditional approaches to human relations and human freedoms. The result has been described as the political triumph of the Right and the cultural triumph of the Left, creating a revolutionary situation in human affairs that some people find exhilarating and many find disorienting.

Apart from disorientation and confusion, one of the most potent responses to the post-traditional society is fundamentalism. Anthony Giddens defines fundamentalists as people who defend tradition in the traditional way.[1] There are important subtleties in the definition. It suggests that it is possible to defend tradition in untraditional ways, to do new things with it, adapt it to contemporary values by re-ordering and re-presenting it in a way that maintains some elements of continuity with the past, while radically repositioning it in the present-day scene. The British monarchy is a useful example, one to which we have already alluded. There is little doubt that it is a tradition that is in crisis in modern Britain. The trend in British society is to move away from inherited privileges, particularly if they are associated with the arrogance of power and its insulation from the challenges of democracy. When people argue for the continuance of the monarchy in Britain today, they argue in untraditional ways. The monarchy had its origins in a social system that was based on dominance by one class over another, with the monarch at the apex of the pyramid of rule. That system has long since been abandoned in theory, though much of what I have called the theatre of the tradition has survived, the monarchy itself being the most conspicuous example. The traditional way to defend the monarchy would be to point to the divine right of monarchs to rule over us by the command of God. Powerful institutions have usually cemented their base by claiming some sort of divine origin, but claims like that only work when they are believed, which is when the tradition is still living, that is to say, when it is one that has the consent of those who are affected by it. No one in Britain today would seriously argue for the retention of the monarchy along these theological lines. They would offer arguments that were largely pragmatic. They might say that there was something to be said for maintaining great historic continuities, other things being equal, though not at any price. They might argue that the monarchy provided us with a useful symbolic representation of the continuity of the nation; that it was a useful tourist attraction; that it helped boost British exports or that it saved us from the huckster-ism of presidential elections. They would not argue that to question the monarchy was to question God or the natural order of things. A fundamentalist defence of the monarchy would be laughed at today, but other forms of fundament-alism still influence our thinking on important issues, such as our freedom to drink, inhale or ingest certain natural substances that have been growing in the planet for a long time. It is a tangled subject, but one way into it is to take a look at the current debate about the medical use of cannabis.

Without, for the moment, taking sides on the question of decriminalising this substance, the dilemma that faces us in the current climate is fascinating. Here is a natural substance that we have decided to ban as a recreational drug. We subsequently discover that, used in certain forms under medical supervision, it has beneficial effects on people suffering from a number of incurable and distressing diseases. Let us take Keith as an example. Keith was infected with HIV in 1983. By 1993 he had developed wasting syndrome, a metabolic change that causes patients to lose rapidly not only fat, but muscle tissue. It is usually a death sentence. In a few months Keith lost forty-five pounds, a quarter of his body weight. Like many people with AIDS, Keith takes ten to fifteen medications a day. Many of them cause debilitating nausea and destroy his appetite, yet many of these drugs are supposed to be taken on a full stomach, and missing one dose can be disastrous. Keith was dying slowly of emaciation when he got into an experimental trial in which wasting syndrome was treated with human growth hormone. For this new drug to work, it was essential to eat three meals a day, something Keith found impossible to do. His physician mentioned to him that many of her patients were inhaling marijuana to suppress nausea and increase their appetite. He began taking a puff or two before eating, enough to give him an appetite without getting stoned. Fortunately, Keith lives in California where, in November 1996, voters overwhelmingly approved Proposition 215 to enable seriously ill people to obtain marijuana upon the recommendation of a physician. Keith regained the weight he had lost, is still eating three meals a day and is the picture of health.[2] It was the growth hormone that put on the weight, but without the marijuana to stimulate his appetite he would be dead today.

Moira, on the other hand, is in a more difficult situation. She suffers from multiple sclerosis, a condition for which there is no cure, but she was advised by knowledgeable friends that eating cannabis cake would considerably alleviate her symptoms. She tried it and found that it did, indeed, provide her with relief in a way no other treatment had. Now she uses it regularly. Unfortunately, Moira lives in Scotland, not California, so she has to break the law to alleviate the symptoms of her condition, and she has to procure her drug through a dealer rather than through a doctor's prescription. A person smoking or eating cannabis ingests at least four hundred different chemicals. Among these are over sixty cannabinoids, the most potent of which is delta-9-tetrahydro-cannabinoid, THC for short. It is THC that may have medical uses. This is why the British Medical Association has recently called for trials with cannabinoids for certain conditions, including multiple sclerosis, spinal chord injuries, cerebral palsy, chronic pain conditions, and as an appetite stimulant for AIDS patients.

Now, even if we support the ban on its use as a recreational drug, what is the moral argument against using cannabis to benefit sick people, such as Keith and Moira, in this way? If we argue that the drug is banned because it harms people, how can we apply that as an argument against using the substance to benefit people? I shall leave on one side for the moment whether we have a right to inhibit people from activities that may endanger them, and stick to the argument over the therapeutic use of a dangerous substance. Many therapeutic agencies can be put to bad uses. Scalpels in the hands of muggers harm people, so we should find ways of denying criminals their possession, but in the hands of surgeons they are instruments of healing. If we ban scalpels completely, because they can be used to injure people, we harm those who would benefit from their therapeutic use. The same is obviously true of substances that can be put to a variety of uses.

The difficulty here may lie in our passion for neatness and absolute systems. Experience teaches that good things can be in contradiction, and the wise approach may be to live with the contradiction, the apparent inconsistency. It would be possible to argue, for instance, that cannabis ought to be banned as a recreational drug because it does harm. The degree of harm would have to be demonstrated, of course, and it would have to be greater than the harm created by denying to people something they feel they have a right to use, but let us assume for the purpose of this argument that the moral argument for criminalising this substance has been conclusively demonstrated. We have done a good thing, therefore, in banning a substance that harms people when used recreationally. But we go on to discover that this same substance, which does harm when used recreationally, also does good, reduces harm, in certain circumstances when carefully prescribed. A mature moral system would learn to live with that apparent contradiction, by recognising that good policies can be in apparent opposition. Indeed, as we have seen, the drama and tragedy of the moral life lies in the fact that most human disagreement is between opposing goods rather than between right and wrong. The most painful element in the debate about drugs is precisely the conflict created by the good of maximising personal freedoms and the good of minimising the harms those freedoms may cause.

The real problem with the debate about drugs is that it takes place across a broad front that prevents us from looking at it in purely moral terms. There is more than an echo here of the ancient culture of sin and witchcraft that held certain substances or natural activities to be wrong in themselves, inherently wicked. The traditional justification for banning these substances would be that they were evil in themselves, and a fundamentalist would probably use language that expressed that superstition. Campaigners against alcohol used to call it *demon drink*, something that was inherently wicked. There is probably an element of that kind of primitive fear at work in the debate about drugs, which is why attitudes to drugs differ widely between the generations. Elderly people are less likely to have used drugs that are in common use among teenagers, preferring the drugs familiarised by their own generation – tobacco and alcohol – to the unknown and therefore more frightening substances used by their grandchildren. There is also, and this is probably the most powerful element in the current debate, the effect of political considerations on moral attitudes. We know that public opinion has a profound influence on politicians, who, apart from wanting to stay in power, cannot be too far ahead of their constituents on controversial topics. And there is the reluctance we have already noticed to recognise the complexity or plural nature of morality, what Isaiah Berlin called the *incommensurability* of values. While we keep all that in our minds, let us try to think about drugs in moral, rather than political, terms and see what conclusions we come to.

Observation suggests that human beings need food, shelter and sex, and they like using drugs in a variety of ways, such as smoking them, chewing them or drinking them. The word 'drug' is loaded, of course, and it is almost impossible to purge it of its unattractive associations. A drug is a natural substance that has psycho-active properties; it works upon the way we feel, and that is why we take it. It may act as an euphoric, putting us in a good, relaxed mood;

it may put us up or put us down, energise or tranquillise us. In other words, it plays with our brain and alters its function. We all seem to have a need to get outside of ourselves from time to time. There are a number of ways of doing this, and religion has been prolific in providing them. Drumming, dancing, chanting are time honoured ways of achieving the state of ecstasy desired, and so is the use of drugs. Humans always seem to have used substances to help them take vacations from the necessary routines of life, but most of us know the difference between a vacation and real life. We need a break from time to time, but we know it is a break, a necessary interruption of the routine, not a commitment to a way of life. We also know that our nature has a tendency to overdo things, to get things out of proportion, so, if we are wise, we learn temperance or moderation; we learn virtue. In the sense defined by Aristotle, a virtue is a mean between two extremes of a good thing. There can be no virtue of an activity that is clearly wrong in itself, such as murder. Virtue applies to things that are good in themselves or morally neutral, but which we can easily abuse, if we are not careful. Virtue lies in finding the mean, the balance, between the two. The virtuous person lives a balanced life. Courage is a good example. In many ways, courage is the foundation virtue. Without it, it is difficult to practise the others. Courage is the mean between cowardice and rashness, the balance between paralysing fear and imprudent recklessness in the face of danger. We can apply the calculus of virtue to our sexuality and other appetites, as well as to the use of those psycho-active substances we use for the pleasure they give us. They are not wrong in themselves, but they can be used wrongly. And this is where the trouble lies.

The drugs that are now illegal substances in Britain and

the USA were gradually outlawed for reasons that have as much to do with politics, class and race as with the problematic qualities of the drugs themselves. If the moral calculus were based simply on the potential danger of any particular drug, then we would long ago have outlawed the two most dangerous drugs on the market: alcohol and tobacco. In Britain, alcohol is involved in 65% of murders, 75% of stabbings, 40% of acts of domestic violence, 30% of acts of child abuse, not to mention the 600 killed and thousands injured annually in drink-drive accidents. There are 1,800 deaths from illegal substances each year, compared with 33,000 that are related to the use of alcohol. In Scotland the figures for drug, alcohol and tobacco related deaths in 1994, a typical year, were, respectively, 247, 720 and 10,420. Against the background of that level of cumulative tragedy, it is not surprising that societies have experimented with banning substances that can wreak such havoc in the human community. The temperate reasonableness of Aristotle's picture of the educated man 'brought up with good habits' is a far cry from kids crazed by crack in inner city ghettoes.

But what happens when something that people want is made illegal? A good example is provided by the great American experiment in prohibition. When something is outlawed that many or most people want, a whole sequence of consequences ensues. First of all, supply drops more than demand, so the price of the substance goes up. Because it has been forced underground, the flow of information necessary to an efficient market is disrupted, so there is less price competition for the drug in demand. The lack of competition enables dealers to charge monopoly prices, so profit margins widen. The big profits attract people who would not otherwise get involved, spreading corruption and contempt for law, and creating opportunities for people who are professionally expert at breaking the law, either criminals or agents of the criminal justice system. The fifth link in the chain is that supply once more becomes conspicuous, marketing the drug becomes more aggressive, the price falls, demand rises, drawing the attention of the forces that got the substance outlawed in the first place. The law cracks down on supply, driving the amateurs out of business and leaving organised crime in control, now with even higher profits and with connections to corrupt members of the law enforcement agencies. At this point the rewards of the illegal traffic attract people capable of marketing it as an institution, and it becomes impossible to eliminate the suppliers. The traffic becomes internationally institutionalised and terrifying in its effects. There seems to be an iron law that the more intense the law enforcement, the more potent the drug becomes. The American experiment with prohibition is the classic case study. It entrenched and institutionalised crime in the USA on a scale that could not previously have been imagined. By the time the Volstead Act was repealed in 1933 the damage was done. That is why the current American war on drugs, with its annual budget of $16 billion dollars, is so familiar to those of us who were brought up on Hollywood movies about Prohibition. We saw the Federal Government lose the war against Al Capone and the syndicates that supplied alcohol to the millions of otherwise law-abiding citizens who wanted it, in spite of the iron rectitude of Elliott Ness and the Untouchables. We are seeing it all again, this time through the lens of movies made about the US Drug Enforcement Agency. We know that those who do not learn from history are destined to go on repeating it, so what lessons can we learn from that great, failed experiment?

The chronology seems fairly clear, even if nothing else is. Until 1916 cocaine and morphine could be bought over the counter at Harrods. As we have seen, the USA led the way in trying to prohibit the use of drugs and alcohol by an amendment to the Constitution in 1919. Tobacco, however, remained untouchable. It was the great American drug, after all, and it was so domesticated and universal that it was impossible to think of it as a drug. Everyone smoked and no one complained. Those old enough to remember will have sat in cinemas for hours pickled in the smoke from hundreds of cigarettes, watching the light from the projection booth cutting its way through a fog that only seemed to add to the romance of the movies. Indeed, the cigarette became an important fashion accessory, the way we expressed our sophistication or punctuated the complex grammar of human interactions. My generation watched Frank Sinatra enter a New York bar in the small hours of the morning, order a drink, push back his Fedora and light a cigarette, all without missing a beat of the song that celebrated the end of yet another love affair. In the monastery in which I was trained for the Christian ministry, any member of the community who wanted it was issued with one and a half ounces of pipe tobacco a week, or the equivalent in cigarettes. It was automatically assumed that everyone smoked. The long reign of King Nicotine illustrates the ancient human failure to connect our own pleasures to those of others. We assume that our pleasures, because they are ours, are more benign and less problematic than the pleasures of strangers. Half the world, for instance, has been consuming hash for centuries, including highly disciplined Islamic countries, which outlaw alcohol, the other domesticated Western drug. It was the very foreignness of hash, though it is arguably less dangerous in its effects than alcohol or tobacco, that made the West suspicious of it. The motive behind American Prohibition seems to have been a potent combination of Puritanism and Racism. Opium was associated with Chinese immigrants, cocaine with southern, black labourers, and alcohol with the Catholic cultures of Europe. The great American war against drugs started in 1919 on a wave of xenophobia.

Britain, to begin with, was more cautious. Since it was recognised that it was not the substances themselves but their abuse that was the problem, an approach to drug abuse was evolved, called the British System. In 1926 the Rolleston Committee report recommended that doctors be permitted to prescribe heroin and cocaine to addicts, and cannabis linctus to patients. The system worked well, though most people were probably unaware of its existence, probably because there were few requests and few addicts, most of whom, in any case, were middle-class or belonged to artistic minorities whose eccentricities were usually tolerated. Anxiety increased in the 1960s when the pattern of drug use changed and became more general. In the USA the association of drugs with the anti-Vietnam War movement probably convinced President Nixon of the un-American nature of many of the substances in question. In Britain in 1962 the Brain Committee recommended no change in the existing practice of allowing doctors to prescribe as they saw fit. However, by 1964 the situation had so deteriorated that the Committee was reconvened to reconsider its decision. It recommended in 1965 that restrictions should be placed on a doctor's right to prescribe heroin and cocaine. This was given the power of law in 1967, along with a requirement for a special Home Office licence to prescribe heroin and cocaine for addiction. Barbiturates and benzodiasapines were added to the list of controlled drugs in 1984 and 1986. The controversial maintenance prescription of substitute drugs, such as methadone, was introduced in the late 1980s in response to the HIV epidemic and was seen as a public health measure. Nowadays heroin addicts, unless they are in the methadone maintenance programme, are dependent on the black market. They turn to theft to buy drugs, and it is the alarming increase of drug related crime that has brought the subject before the general public. A related fact is the link between drug consumption and social deprivation, and the devastating way each reinforces the other. According to one anti-prohibitionist campaigner, 'Whether it is tobacco, alcohol or crack, the link between social deprivation and problematic drug use is very clear. Poor people with little job training, hopes of employment or educational opportunities are living in a state of despair – and heroin is one hell of a drug for dealing with that.'[3] Interestingly, it is a combination of the front line workers in the field – doctors, social workers and the more thoughtful law enforcement officers – who are helping us to rethink out attitude to drugs. Though heroin addicts are relatively few in number, they are uniquely unsympathetic characters who create a disproportionate amount of chaos around them. The tragic heart of the debate is over what to do with them. The only models on offer for dealing with this human tragedy are prohibition, with the consequences we have already noted, or a maintenance programme for addicts that is being increasingly followed in other countries, such as Switzerland. During an experimental three-year period there, when heroin was prescribed for addicts, crime was reduced by 60%, the general and nutritional health of the addicts improved, as did their living conditions, their illicit cocaine and heroin use was dramatically reduced and the number of participants who were employed doubled.[4] The chances are good that in Britain an increasingly experimental approach will be adopted to what seems to be an intractable problem. The purely prohibitionist approach does not seem to work, though the motivation behind it is understandable and it has enormous symbolic importance for many people. On the other hand, an entirely libertarian approach, which may be philosophically attractive to a certain kind of mind, may trap us in the law of unintended consequences, by exposing weaker members of our society to dangers through which the more balanced among us find it possible to navigate without too much risk.

Let me offer some kind of summary, not so much of the argument as of the situation that provokes the argument. Whether we approve or not, it seems to be the case that most people like to use drugs, euphoric or mind-altering substances, because of the pleasure they derive from doing so. However, some people misuse these substances all of the time and many people misuse them some of the time, to a greater or lesser extent. There are people, for example, who become addicted to a particular substance or a cocktail of substances. Experts make a distinction between the physically and psychologically addictive properties of a substance. I suspect that this can never be an absolute distinction, but we are told, for instance, that alcohol is physically addictive; heroin, methadone and nicotine are both physically and psychologically addictive; while cannabis may be psychologically addictive if used heavily. There are mysteries here. Regular use of nicotine seems to produce physical dependence in most users, which is why it is so difficult to give up, while regular use of alcohol clearly addicts some but not most users. However we account for it, there seems to be a significant minority of the population who are unable to use these substances virtuously or moderately. For them the only safe route is total abstention, though moving from addiction to freedom can be crucifyingly difficult and calls for great courage and an enduring discipline. The plight of the addict is enormously resonant in our society and associates many of these substances with images of tragedy and terror that influence our attitude to the best way to order their use. We also know that, although addiction is no respecter of social class, substance abuse amplifies already existing social deprivations and tightens the trap in which the excluded find themselves. And lurking in the deep background is a hangover of metaphysical assumptions about the uniquely fallen status of certain pleasure-yielding substances that makes it difficult for us to view them neutrally and plan their use dispassionately.

It is not surprising, therefore, that the prohibitionist approach has been so potent in our history. For some people personal prohibition is the only policy that will save their lives, so it is easy to see how society as a whole could extrapolate this approach as the best way to deal with the threat that drug abuse poses for the civil order. The flaw in the prohibitionist approach, however, is that it seems to be inconsistent with some of the other values we prize in an open society. This is an example of the way good values frequently conflict in a democratic polity. It is clearly a good thing to want to protect vulnerable people from the consequences of certain behaviours, but it is also a good thing to allow responsible people maximum freedom, within acceptable limits, to manage their lives according to their own desires. The difficulty with the prohibitionist approach is that it places these two values in irresolvable conflict with each other. It is also arguable that laws that prohibit activities and substances that many people want access to, at least some of the time, can only be applied successfully in totalitarian systems where those in power have no respect for individual freedoms. In open societies prohibitions that do not have the overwhelming consent of the people are almost impossible to police, and can end up corrupting the very system that is there to enforce them. The main value of prohibitionist laws lies in the symbolic disapproval they express of certain behaviours. In open societies they seem to be incapable of extirpating them.

Fortunately, the prohibitionist approach is not the only model we have available to us. There is a middle way between absolute prohibition and absolute license and we are already following it in our management of legal drugs. The history of tobacco use is a good example of this process. In the early part of this century, as we have already noted, tobacco use was widespread and socially acceptable. There was always a struggle to keep children from smoking, but as soon as they were old enough most people went on to cigarettes, or pipe tobacco in the case of some men. Those innocent days are over. Once the link between tobacco and disease was established, a strategy started to evolve that was designed to educate people about the dangers of smoking. We went from health warnings on packets of cigarettes to the banning of advertising and the prohibition of smoking in many public places, which is why cigarette smokers can now be seen standing uncomfortably in doorways having a quick puff before ascending to their smoke-free offices. And, of course, we tax tobacco punitively, thereby illustrating one of the necessary hypocrisies of government: actively discouraging smoking, while raising vast tax revenues from the very people of whom it affects to disapprove. In all these areas, adults will calculate the risks and benefits of smoking differently, and there are striking differences between different cultures. The United States, which still carries many vestiges of its puritan past, has made smoking tobacco almost impossible except behind closed doors in private, while in parts of Europe most of the population go on smoking, balancing, presumably, the pleasure it gives them against its cumulative effect on their health.

An obverse development can be traced in the history of alcohol consumption in our society. In the Scotland of my boyhood there existed a strange combination of grudging legal access to alcohol alongside a semi-prohibitionist culture that limited its availability in arbitrary ways. For example, it was impossible to get a drink in a pub on a Sunday, because they were not allowed to open, while a bona fide traveller could buy a drink in a hotel. In my community in the west of Scotland this led to the phenomenon of the Sunday bus run to country hotels for the simple purpose of consuming alcohol. A bus would be hired to take the customers to a series of hotels in the district, and these bona fide travellers would return to their families at the end of the day much more heavily intoxicated than might have been the case if they had been able to go down to their local bar for a drink or two after lunch. Opening hours during the week were also severely limited. The average Scottish pub was an austere, male dominated establishment, designed for heavy drinking under the tyrannous eye of the clock. Recent changes in the culture of drinking in Scotland have increasingly civilised the consumption of alcohol. Alcohol abuse is still a major problem in Britain, but it is not the ugly and brutal thing it was in the Scotland of my boyhood, when the streets of most cities after closing time on Friday and Saturday nights were filled with drunk men, staggering home to their frightened wives and children. Of course, social development creates new problems from old habits, and the lethal combination of drinking and driving is one we are now tackling. In time it will probably be made illegal to drive with any level of alcohol in the bloodstream, a form of prohibition that society will probably tolerate.

This swift survey illustrates the dynamic nature of societies as they struggle with the impact of human appetites upon the common good. The process never stops, though certain elements seem to endure. Human nature has a tendency to hedonistic inflation, to turn good or neutral things into bad by using them excessively. This tendency to overdo things is greatly amplified in some people and it is strongly influenced by psycho-social factors that are difficult to control. In making the ethical calculus, therefore, there emerges a tension between the educated freedom of the virtuous person who is taught the wisdom of moderation, and the need to protect the weak, especially the young, from the perils of this same freedom. The balance is never perfectly achieved anywhere – it is always something that is in process – but moments arise when a particular combination of circumstances calls for a new level of honesty in our address upon the subject, as well as a deeper investigation of all the factors involved. We seem to have reached one of those moments in our own time. We are experiencing an uncomfortable confusion in an area that connects personal morality and private freedom with the public good. History teaches that the best way to handle this kind of dilemma is to acknowledge that the moral calculus rarely affords us absolutely clear guidance in arbitrating complex human choices. Limiting the harm that the abuse of natural substances can cause us is a laudable aim, but it is in conflict with our freedom to use these substances, even to our own harm, if we so wish. The more important point is the need to protect the freedom of humanity to live life in its own way, provided it is not thereby invading the equal rights of others or damaging their freedoms or interests. We should think long and hard, therefore, before prohibiting something that people want, just because we disapprove of it. We should also learn to make connections between our own customs and preferences and the customs and preferences of others of which we may disapprove for no stronger reason than that they differ from our own. The positive protection of the freedom of others to live their own lives in their own way is the strongest moral argument against prohibition. It is a point of view that is increasingly prevalent in our society, though it is in conflict with residual elements of the old command systems. People were ordered around in previous eras, because that is what happened in domination systems. People were told what to do and what not to do, because that was the tradition, the way things were done. We have moved far from those days, but there are still many remnants of the old order around, particularly in the area of human sexuality and the use of drugs. Attempts are sometimes made to argue in untraditional ways to preserve the traditional prohibitions, but the unspoken arguments are the potent ones, and they tend to be based on the old irrational taboos. In open, democratic societies, however, it is impossible to impose, let alone to police, moral systems that are based on traditional principles that are no longer accepted. That is why there is more than an element of farce in the current debate about sex and drugs in our society. Mother and father are tucked up in bed in the attic reading their prohibitionist tracts, while their children in the basement are experimenting with stuff their parents have not even heard of. The only way to bring rationality and order into the situation is to acknowledge it and try to manage the consequences. But even if the argument from the positive moral importance of freedom is not persuasive, the costly failure of prohibition provides us with a strong negative reason for thinking again.

CHAPTER FIVE

Life Wars

The trouble with life is that we understand it backwards, but have to live it forwards. We keep moving through life trying to figure it out as we go along, living experimentally, trying out different attitudes and theories, changing our minds, reversing ourselves sometimes, sometimes coming back to where we were at the beginning. In my own case, for example, one of my major conflicts has been over the kind of people I have found myself admiring. For most boys, physical courage is an important and admirable value. Boys of my generation were brought up on adventure stories about situations that called for great courage in the hero. Since I went to the cinema more enthusiastically than I went to school, I imbibed the great myth in the classic Western film of the lonely hero riding into town, defending it against the local bad guys, a few of whom he reluctantly but professionally kills, with little help from the townsfolk, before riding off into the sunset.

Physical courage still seems to me to be an admirable virtue. That is why I continue to admire boxers, though I am ambivalent about the morality of boxing. Most of us fear pain and try to avoid it; it makes us physical cowards, people who submit to another's strength, because we are afraid that if we challenge it we'll be hurt. Boxers train themselves to accept the pain, to endure the constant hurt. There is a famous photograph of the Irish boxer Barry McGuigan on the stool before the last round of the fight in which he lost his world title. He has that deep, black, faraway look in the eyes of someone who is enduring unbelievable pain long, long after the normal, cowardly person, would have given in. I admire the same virtue in soldiers who train themselves to face death. I even find myself admiring mercenaries, the wild geese among men, who sell their courage to those who will pay for it. That is why I like A.E. Housman's 'Epitaph on an Army of Mercenaries'.

> These, in the days when heaven was falling,
>   The hour when earth's foundations fled,
> Followed their mercenary calling,
>   And took their wages and are dead.
>
> Their shoulders held the sky suspended;
>   They stood, and earth's foundations stay;
> What God abandoned, these defended,
>   And saved the sum of things for pay.

Sometimes an account of courage unto death can bring tears to the eyes, as the story of Haing Ngor did to mine recently. He was the actor who survived the Khmer Rouge in Cambodia, escaped to the USA and then appeared in *The Killing Fields*, the magnificent film that was made about that horrifying episode in twentieth-century history. During the terror in Cambodia his wife, pregnant with their child, had died in prison and the only thing of hers he possessed was her photograph, which he kept in a gold locket round his neck. Some time ago he was held up by a street gang in Los Angeles and shot, because he refused to hand the locket over to them. That is a story of powerful love, as well as enormous courage, the refusal to give up the only reminder of the great passion of a brave man's life.

My dilemma as a young man was that I continued to

admire and fantasise about men of courage, and the violence they perpetrated and endured, long after I had committed myself to a contrary way, the way of peace and non-violence, the way of Jesus. This was before I had really discovered the intense physical and political courage of Jesus, so I was caught between a heroic and a religious understanding of life; and only now am I beginning to see that this is a false dilemma. I was enormously attracted to the heroic, Homeric approach to life of men of courage and passion 'who sang the sun in flight', in Dylan Thomas's words, men who ate and drank and fought and made love and died bravely. They mourned the brevity of their lives, but refused to compromise their heroic virtue in order to prolong it. I continued to admire these types of men long after I had put on the cassock and embraced the kind of religion that Nietzsche dismissed as weak and world-denying, because it seemed to fight against the heroic virtues and imposed a discipline that denied the life-force in men. The dilemma that increasingly tormented me was not so much personal as philosophical. It is true that, like most people, I found it difficult to deny my appetites and sublimate them into spirituality and service of others, but I now see that the conflict was there at the theoretical level as well. Did I actually believe that a world purged of the need for heroic virtues (even if it could be achieved) would be a better world? In a world where the lion lay down with the lamb, what would have happened to the fierce glory of the lion's nature? In a world purged of conflict and danger, what would become of the virtue of courage and that heart-stopping bravery that defies death itself? My admiration for these virtues saw them as good, as worthy of my admiration, approval and imitation, even though they appeared to be in conflict with the system I had embraced.

Now I know that it is that little word 'system' that causes
the trouble. A system is a unified view of life, an artificial
harmonisation, an attempt (always violent – whether physical, intellectual or both) to impose order upon chaos.
People of the Bible have been taught to fear chaos. Chaos
suggests to us riot, confusion and disorder. Interestingly,
that is not at all its original sense. It is a Greek word that
means void, emptiness, abyss. It is out of this abyss of
nothingness that God brings creation, according to the first
chapter of Genesis. 'And the earth was waste and void; and
darkness was upon the face of the deep: and the spirit of
God moved upon the face of the waters.' God brings
profusion out of emptiness, the extravagance of creation
out of the barrenness of chaos; but we seem to have a
passion for reversing the process and restoring an ordered
void; we want to impose system upon the prodigal variety
of actual life, force it on to the Procustean bed of a single
template. One of the ways we do this is in our constant
search for a unified value system. We do it in all sorts of
other ways, of course. When the British had an empire they
imposed the template of their culture on the very different
traditions they found in Africa, Asia, Australasia and the
Americas. This kind of imperialism has been generally true
of Christianity, which has believed, at various times in its
history, that all other religions are false and lead to damna-
tion. Even within our own moral culture we try to impose
system and order, because something in us fears the void.

I understand now that my confusion in struggling between the Homeric and the Christian attitudes to life was
not because it was a choice between right and wrong, good
and bad, but because it was a choice between incommen-
surable or irreconcilable goods. To recognise this is finally
to understand the fundamentally tragic nature of many of

our choices, even of life itself. The thinker who confronted this reality with the greatest courage and clarity was Isaiah Berlin. He wrote:

> If we are not armed with an a priori guarantee of the proposition that a total harmony of true values is somewhere to be found, we must fall back on the ordinary resources of empirical observation and ordinary human knowledge. And these certainly give us no warrant for supposing that all good things, or all bad things for that matter, are reconcilable with each other. The world that we encounter in ordinary experience is one in which we are faced with choices between ends equally ultimate, and claims equally absolute, the realisation of some of which must inevitably involve the sacrifice of others. Indeed, it is because this is their situation that men place such immense value upon the freedom to choose; for if they had assurance that in some perfect state, realisable by men on earth, no ends pursued by them would ever be in conflict, the necessity and agony of choice would disappear, and with it the central importance of the freedom to choose. Any method of bringing this final state nearer would then seem fully justified, no matter how much freedom were sacrificed to forward its advance.
>
> It is, I have no doubt, some such dogmatic certainty that has been responsible for the deep, serene, unshakeable conviction in the minds of some of the most merciless tyrants and persecutors in history that what they did was fully justified by its purpose . . . But equally it seems to me that the belief that some single formula can in principle be found whereby all the diverse ends of men can be harmoniously realised is demonstrably false. If, as I believe, the ends of men are many, and not all of them are in principle compatible with each other, then the possibility of conflict – and of tragedy – can never wholly be eliminated from human life, either personal or social. The necessity of choosing between absolute claims is then an inescapable characteristic of the human condition.[1]

John Gray has summed up Berlin's account of moral pluralism under three main characteristics. First of all, it is a rejection of the idea of a perfect society or even a perfect human life. Life is manifold in the forms it takes; it is gloriously and inescapably plural. It follows that a developed morality cannot have a hierarchical structure that decides practical dilemmas by the application of a system of principles. In life we are in the business of making trade-offs between conflicting goods and evils, and there is no infallible measuring system for weighing these values against each other. That is why we often reach situations where further reflective deliberation gets us no further and we have no choice but to act.[2] I am reminded of Denis Healey's statement that in politics one never reaches conclusions, but one must make decisions.

I have offered that prologue on the clash of values, and the impossibility of harmonising them into a universal system, because it may help to steady our nerves as we enter the war zone where disputes about the beginning and ending of life are conducted today. Here we are confronted by irreconcilable approaches that go on battling one another, like those ancient wars of religion or those intractable ethnic conflicts that litter our history. Abortion is probably the issue that generates the most heat, so let us open the discussion by looking at some of the prevailing attitudes to this hot topic. There seem to be several groups in the abortion debate, so we can talk about a continuum or spectrum of views. The ones at each end of the line seem to be in irreconcilable opposition, but there is a position close to the centre that seems able to keep in touch with the more extreme opinions without necessarily sharing them. Before looking at them, let me repeat the point I have just made. Most of the conflicts we engage in are between opposing goods, conflicting values, rather than between straight right and wrong. This does not mean that we will refuse to take a stand, make a decision, go for one of the options in a particular conflict, but it ought to moderate our appetite for dismissing those who are opposed to us on the grounds that they are immoral or have no sense of values. Another issue that will confront us is how we manage these intractable disagreements in a plural culture. As I have already observed, most of us probably feel that somewhere beyond argument there is a unified theory of human nature and its values and that if we all struggle hard enough we'll find it. Both experience and reflection contradict that. This, however, is not moral relativism. It is not the same thing at all as saying that one attitude is no better or worse than any other. To say that values conflict with each other is not to say that there are no values at all, no fundamental principles that characterise us as human. Our tragedy is not that we are indifferent to the good, but that we recognise that it is sometimes in conflict with itself. Berlin is quite clear that pluralism of the sort he describes is not the same thing as absolute moral relativism.

> If I say of someone that he is kind or cruel, loves truth or is indifferent to it, he remains human in either case. But if I find a man to whom it literally makes no difference whether he kicks a pebble or kills his family, since either would be an antidote to ennui or inactivity, I shall not be disposed, like consistent relativists, to attribute to him merely a different code of morality from my own or that of most men, but shall begin to speak of insanity and inhumanity; I shall be inclined to consider him mad; which is a way of saying that I do not regard such a being as being fully a man at all. It is cases of this kind, which seem to make it clear that ability to recognise universal – or almost universal – values enters into our analysis of such fundamental

*concepts as 'man', 'rational', 'sane', 'natural', which are usually
thought of as descriptive and not evaluative.*[3]

The difficulty we face in discussing abortion is not that we
see obviously good people consistently battling against
obviously wicked people, but that different moral traditions
offer different answers to certain basic questions, and there
is no external arbiter to whom we can go to settle the
dispute. For instance, if we ask the basic question, 'When
does human life begin?', we get a number of different
answers. The Roman Catholic tradition holds that life
begins at conception. According to the Jewish tradition,
life starts at the eighth week of gestation, when the embryo
is fully formed. Others have proposed that the beginning of
life is at implantation in the womb; yet others that it begins
in the second week after conception, when the primitive
neural tube is formed and the embryo may respond to
stimuli. Some say that, since life has been defined as being
terminated when brain activity ends, it should therefore be
considered that life begins when brain activity starts. And
others hold that human life begins when the conceptus
becomes a person with some degree of sentience or active
volition.

However, the philosopher John Harris argues that there
is an important distinction to be noticed here. He writes:

*Many people have supposed that the answer to the question 'when
does life begin to matter morally?' is the same as the answer to the
question 'when does life begin?' The moment of conception may
seem to be the obvious answer to the question of when life begins.
But of course the egg is alive well before conception . . . the sperm
too is alive and wriggling. Life is a continuous process that
proceeds uninterrupted from generation to generation continu-
ously evolving. It is not, then, that life begins at conception. But if*

not life, is it not at least the new individual that begins at conception?[4]

He points out that life is a continuum and that the emergence of the individual occurs gradually. All that can safely be said of the fertilised egg is that it is live human tissue. In other words, life does not begin at fertilisation, it continues, so what we need is an account of when life begins to matter morally. Harris claims that it is the capacity to value one's own life that is crucial morally. He writes:

> In order to value its own life a being would have to be aware that it has a life to value. This would at the very least require something like Locke's conception of self-consciousness, which involves a person's being able to 'consider itself as itself in different times and places'. Self-consciousness is not simple awareness, rather it is awareness of awareness. To value its own life, a being would have to be aware of itself as an independent centre of consciousness, existing over time with a future that it was capable of envisaging and wishing to experience.[5]

In this way Harris arrives at what he calls the concept of the person, as any being capable of valuing its own existence. The moral difference between a person and a non-person, therefore, lies in the value that people give to their own lives. The reason it is wrong to kill a person is that to do so takes from her something she values, as well as the very thing that makes it possible for her to value anything at all. Harris claims that to kill a person not only frustrates her wishes for her own future, but frustrates every wish she has. He goes on:

> Creatures that cannot value their own existence cannot be wronged in this way, for their death deprives them of nothing

they can value. Of course, non-persons can be harmed in other
ways, by being subjected to pain for example, and there are good
reasons for avoiding subjecting sentient creatures to pain if this
can be avoided.[6]

Following the logic of this definition, Harris argues that since the fetus is not a person in the sense he has defined, a woman has a right to choose an abortion. Since it is not a person, the fetus cannot be wronged if its life is ended prematurely, though it can be wronged in other ways, if it is caused pain, for example. This is why he argues that it is important that abortion is painless for the fetus.

At the opposite end of the continuum to Harris in this debate are those who argue that the fetus is a helpless unborn child, so that permitting abortion is permitting murder. This view, like the position argued by John Harris, has the virtue of absolute clarity, which is why it attracts so many. It seems capable of removing the anguish that characterises the debate. After all, if it is strongly believed that the fetus has the moral status of a person, then to deprive it of life is the crime of murder. The difficulty with this widely held view, however, is that inconsistencies begin to creep in when we examine it closely, as Ronald Dworkin did in his book, *Life's Dominion.*[7] He points out that even those conservatives who believe that the law should pro- hibit abortion because it is murder permit certain excep- tions. For instance, they now say that abortion should be permitted to save the mother's life. Dworkin says that this exception is inconsistent with any belief that the fetus is a person with a right to live, because very few people believe that it is morally justifiable for a third party, even a doctor, to kill one innocent person to save another. However, the extreme Roman Catholic position has the virtue of absolute consistency in this area. In a popular novel, *The Cardinal*, later turned into a movie, the central character is a priest who is called upon, as the next of kin, to decide whether to save his sister's life by permitting the medical team to abort her late-term baby or let his sister die in order to save the unborn child. He sticks to his belief that it would be immoral to kill the unborn child even to save the life of the mother, and refuses the abortion, in spite of the anguish it brings him,. The child is born safely and his sister dies in the process. Few people would make that choice today, but it is the inescapable consequence of the absolute belief that the fetus is a person with rights that cannot be abrogated even to save the life of another. The permission to abort in order to save the mother's life is the most obvious exception made by otherwise conservative opponents of abortion, but they do make other exceptions to the absolute rule, such as accepting abortion after rape or incest. Dworkin writes:

> The more such exceptions are allowed, the clearer it becomes that conservative opposition to abortion does not presume that a fetus is a person with a right to live. It would be contradictory to insist that a fetus has a right to live that is strong enough to justify prohibiting abortion even when childbirth would ruin a mother's or a family's life but that it ceases to exist when the pregnancy is the result of sexual crime of which the fetus is, of course, wholly innocent.[8]

Dworkin believes that any exceptions to the absolute and full human rights of the fetus that permit abortion, however grave the context, demonstrate an implicit acceptance that the fetus does not, in fact, have the full moral status of personhood. It is this gap in their practice that allows him to offer a mediating position that recognises the morally problematic nature of abortion without ruling it out absolutely in all circumstances. This is why he goes on to offer what he calls a liberal view of abortion, one that I would prefer to call a middle way between the absolute prohibitionists and those such as John Harris for whom abortion is not morally problematic at all, provided it is humanely administered. What Dworkin calls the paradigm liberal position has four parts. First of all, it rejects the extreme position that abortion is morally unproblematic. It insists that abortion is always a grave moral decision, certainly after the genetic individuality of the fetus is established and it has successfully implanted in the womb, normally after fourteen days. From that point on, he believes, abortion involves a serious moral cost, because it means the extinction of a human life that has already begun, so it should never be permissible for trivial or frivolous reasons, such as, for instance, to avoid cancelling a vacation.

His second point is that abortion can, nevertheless, be morally justified for a variety of serious reasons. He argues that it is justified to save the life of the mother and in cases of rape or incest, as well as in cases where severe fetal abnormality has been diagnosed that make it likely that the child, if carried to term, will have only a brief, painful and frustrating life. He amplifies this position, by adding that it may even be argued that, in the face of severe fetal abnormality, abortion is not only morally permitted but may be morally required, because it would be wrong knowingly to bring such a child into the world.

He goes on to argue, in his third point, that a woman's concern for her own interests is also an adequate justification for abortion, if the consequences of giving birth would be permanent and grave for her family's life. He writes:

Depending on the circumstances, it may be permissible for her to abort her pregnancy if she would otherwise have to leave school or

give up a chance for a career or a satisfying and independent life.
For many women these are the most difficult cases, and people
who take the paradigm liberal view would assume that the
expectant mother would suffer some regret if she decided to abort.
But they would not condemn the decision as selfish; on the
contrary, they might well suppose that the contrary decision
would be a serious moral mistake.[9]

The fourth strand in this narrative is the political opinion
that the state has no business intervening even to prevent
morally impermissible abortions, because the question is
ultimately for the women who carries the fetus to decide.
Others may disapprove, and be right to do so. The law
might even oblige the woman to discuss her decision with
others, but the state, in the end, must let her decide for
herself; it must not impose other people's moral convictions
upon her and her body. I would like to suggest that a purely
pragmatic reason for supporting this particular point of
view is the historical knowledge that when abortions are
legally prohibited they do not cease, but they do become
unsafe and frequently lethal. This is why many people who
dislike abortion may prefer to have it made safely available
rather than attempted in secret by unskilled practitioners, or
be self-induced.

The point of view reflected by these four components
seems to be widely shared and is more or less the basis upon
which the Abortion Act in Britain was formulated. It plies a
middle way between those for whom abortion is never
morally problematic and those for whom it is always and in
every circumstance murder. It follows that those who
follow this middle way become less comfortable the further
into the pregnancy the woman has gone. Most people seem
to believe that early abortions are less morally problematic
than later ones, which is one reason why it has recently

been suggested that it might be worth making it easier for a woman to have an early abortion than the present Act does. The logic in this is obvious. If we reject the view that the fetus is a full human person, but are equally uncomfortable with the opposing view that the fetus has no personal status at all, so that aborting it is morally unproblematic, then we probably hold the view that there is something incremental about the moral status of the fetus, so that the closer it comes to term the more problematic abortion becomes. This is why, for instance, the Jewish tradition would find nothing morally problematic about aborting up to the eighth week of gestation. Nevertheless, those who find themselves in this position are likely to experience a certain moral discomfort. This is because those who hold what Dworkin calls the pardigm liberal position believe that, while abortion may morally be permitted, it remains morally problematic. Why do we agonise over abortion more than over, say, an appendectomy or tonsillectomy? It is because we believe that human life in the fetal state, while it may not have the full moral status of personhood with all its rights and responsibilities, nevertheless has intrinsic value and moral significance. We may prefer the risks and dangers of choice to the risks and dangers of prohibition, but we continue to recognise that abortion is problematic, because it is irresponsible to waste human life without a justification of appropriate importance. However, the earlier the choice is made, the less problematic it feels. It seems likely that science will soon alter the focus of the debate on the termination of pregnancy by moving it from the surgical interventions of abortion, and its inescapably public and legal dimension, into the private area of the chemistry of birth control. Recent medical advances are revolutionising a woman's choices when confronted with an unwanted pregnancy. A woman can now buy an early pregnancy test kit and test herself. If she is pregnant and wishes to end the pregnancy, she can get a prescription from her doctor for what is essentially a chemical abortion performed within the first six weeks of pregnancy. Following this method allows women to control their own reproductive lives and to take action immediately if they have had unprotected sex. If it became the norm, it would greatly reduce the number of surgical abortions performed. Just as importantly, it would return the matter to the private lives of the women involved and allow them the dignity of making their own choices and acting upon them without leaving their own personal environment.

At the moment, however, prevailing medical practice brings us right up against one of those classic human dilemmas between irreconcilable choices. Abortion wastes the value of human life and is therefore a moral wrong, but we permit it because sometimes the intrinsic value of other human lives would be wasted in a decision against abortion. This is precisely the dilemma that faces us as we think about the fourteen-year-old girl in the no-hope housing estate contemplating the birth of an unwanted baby. One way of handling that ethical calculus is to measure the waste of a life that has already been lived for fourteen years and would be wrecked by having the baby, against the waste involved in aborting an early-stage fetus in whose life human investment has so far been negligible. Liberal opinion cares more for lives that are being lived now than about the possibility of other lives to come. Nevertheless, the choices are tragic, not easy, and those who make them should not be condemned because their moral calculus differs from our own. Emotions are easily roused in this debate, but emotions, though they can dupe us, may also help to keep us sensitive. I have used the word 'tragic' frequently in this chapter, because it captures the intractability of the competing values that face us here. I regret it when either side in the abortion debate assumes the moral high-ground, so that prohibitionists give the impression that those who believe in choice have no moral basis for their point of view and are little more than murderers; while pro-choicers sometimes give the impression that abortion is as morally unproblematic as a tonsillectomy. This is why some of us feel acutely uncomfortable in positioning ourselves at either end of the continuum and prefer, however agonisingly, to pick our way with considerable care through the middle of the battlefield.

Handling the politics of abortion is a real test of the maturity of a pluralist moral culture. What can a group do that believes there is never any moral justification for abortion and that all abortion is murder, in a society where theirs is not the majority view? They have a right to debate with the rest of us, but they should be careful about the tone they use in their arguments. To suggest that theirs is the only morally serious position, and that only they have any reverence for human life, is demeaning to those of us who have wrestled with the issue and reach, however uncomfortably, different conclusions. The abortion debate provides us with an example of how uncomfortable certain groups can be in modern, secular, pluralist cultures. We are seeing something of the same discomfort in the increasing call for state-supported sectarian schools. It is difficult for intact moral and religious communities to live alongside their secular neighbours, especially if they belong to traditions that have had a long history of cultural dominance in certain places at certain times. Those who adhere to monist moral systems find it difficult to adjust to life in pluralist cultures, and they usually claim that pluralist cultures have no values of their own. In fact, there are many important values that underpin pluralist systems, none more important than freedom and respect for the human rights of others. One of the paradoxes of this debate is that the systems that monists look back at nostalgically often showed scant respect for human life and individual rights. One of the ugliest aspects of the Christian Right in the USA, with its strong pro-life ethic, is the way it enthusiastically endorses capital punishment. There never have been perfect human societies. Our society today is certainly not perfect, and there is much about it that is ugly and spiritually deadening. Even so, I'd rather be in a society that lived with the unpredictable consequences of giving people great freedom of choice than in one that told them all exactly what to do and think, especially if it is claimed that all the orders come directly from God.

The question of whether it is ever justified to help people to end their life because it has become an intolerable burden to them is another area where we face opposing goods rather than a straight choice between good and evil, right and wrong. Obviously, the principle of consent is fundamentally important here, but people who oppose euthanasia under any circumstances are usually afraid that if it were made legal it would put pressure on aged and terminally ill people to decide upon a matter that would not otherwise occur to them. There are important distinctions to be made in this debate, as in the debate about abortion. The positions at each end of the debate, one that forbids any kind of medical management that compromises the duty to keep people alive and the other that sees nothing morally problematic in assisted suicide, are less likely to help us in addressing the complexity of the situations that face us than the kind of calculus we followed in our discussion of abortion. Most people, even if they are sympathetic towards those who ask for assistance in ending their own lives, would admit that there is something morally problematic about assisting at another's suicide. The result of thinking round the subject might lead them to the conclusion that it would be morally justified to offer such assistance, but the discomfort they would feel in arriving at such a conclusion is itself evidence of the morally problematic nature of the issue. It is right that we should feel such discomfort, because it can never be morally uncontentious to assist in the death of another, even with her consent. By the same token, it would be difficult to argue that there are never any circumstances in which it would be morally permissible to help someone to die in this way. The circumstances would have to be acute before such a decision could be justified, of course, but it is not impossible to come up with examples. An obvious example would be of someone being burned at the stake during the era of religious and political persecution. Screaming in agony in the searing flames, it would be morally justified to accede to the victim's plea and end his life immediately, if we had the means to do so, such as with an accurately fired shot from a rifle. An intervention like that would be a true example of mercy killing and, tragic though it would be, it would be morally justifiable. There have been incidents from medicine that have come close to such an extreme example, but they invariably create more than a moral dilemma for the doctor who responds to them.

We know that, in modern medicine, pain management is extremely subtle, though it is not necessarily universally effective. In most cases doctors are able to manage terrible illnesses in a way that makes the pain bearable or eliminates it altogether. However, the application of the necessary levels of the painkilling drugs invariably shortens the life of the patient and, in effect, kills her. This is usually described as the law of second effect. The primary intention is to banish the pain, not end the life, but the secondary effect of the main intention is to shorten the life of the patient. We could dismiss this distinction as specious, arguing robustly that it would be better to declare honestly that we are, however incrementally, shortening the life of the patient. The doctor in question, however, is likely to insist on the distinction, because on it hangs an important legal point. There was a celebrated case involving a doctor some years ago that makes the point exactly. Nigel Cox had been Lilian Boyes' doctor for thirteen years. They had a close personal relationship, and he had promised her that she would not suffer as she got to the end of her agonising illness. Unfortunately, the painkilling medicine he had counted on failed, and she begged him to kill her. He injected her with a lethal dose of potassium chloride, and she died within minutes. He scrupulously reported the injection in her medical records, and a Catholic nurse who discovered the report informed the hospital authorities. Because the body had already been cremated and there was no evidence that the drug had actually killed her, he was tried for attempted murder. His lawyer argued that he had given her potassium chloride only to relieve her suffering, but the jury disagreed, because the drug had no analgesic effect, and found him guilty. The judge sentenced him to one year, with the sentence suspended. People on both sides of the question were outraged, some that he had been treated so leniently, others that he had been convicted at all for performing an act of compassionate friendship. It is argu-able that had Doctor Cox found a drug of sufficient analgesic power to remove Mrs Boyes's pain it might also have ended her life in doing so, but his defence of secondary effect would probably have worked with the jury, had a criminal prosecution even been initiated. There is clearly an important legal distinction between administering drugs that shorten life, but whose primary purpose is to control pain, and administering drugs aimed solely at ending it. There is probably also an important moral distinction between them, but it is not as wide as we are tempted to make out. Doctors usually know that they are shortening the lives of their patients by their management of certain terminal conditions, so it could be argued that they are practising incremental euthanasia. Nevertheless, there is an important distinction in their intention for the patient, between easing their last days and consciously setting out to end them. And, as we have seen, it is a distinction that the law acknowledges as important.

We are confronted with different, though related difficulties, when patients demand that life support systems be removed, even when they are not dying, because they find life intolerable in the circumstances in which they must live it. In an important Canadian decision in January 1992 a Quebec judge, Mr Justice Dufour, ruled that people had this right. Nancy B, a twenty-five-year-old victim of a rare neurological disease called Guillain-Barre syndrome, and paralysed from the neck down, asked the doctor to turn off the respirator that kept her alive. Her doctor advised her that she could live on the respirator for years, but she wanted to die. 'The only thing I have is looking at television and looking at the walls. It's enough. It's two and a half years that I've been on this thing and I think I've done my share.'[10] The judge said he would be very happy if Nancy changed her mind, but he understood her wishes, and granted her request. The respirator was withdrawn, and Nancy died in February 1992.

Subtly different though they are, these examples show that there is clearly a significant moral barrier between allowing someone to die, even actively withdrawing them from a support machine, and actually and actively killing them. It is an ancient and well-founded distinction, and one which most people in society are understandably reluctant to tamper with. Because humans are not inhibited from killing one another by instinct, we need the strongest possible cultural inhibitions against killing. Many people argue that active euthanasia would gradually erode this inhibition. The antithesis to this point of view, however, is created by the person in unbearable pain, such as the man being burned at the stake; or Lilian Boyes, whose condition seemed beyond the reach of conventional medical management and who asked a trusted physician to give her the relief of a dignified end. The principle of reverence for the sacredness of life struggles with the principle of compassion towards a particular individual in unbearable agony. It is doubtful if any law could cover such human complexity, but it may be that there ought to be a principle that affirms the law but allows carefully negotiated exceptions to it. Unless something like this happens, dedicated and compassionate physicians like Dr Cox will continue to find themselves in terrible dilemmas, and their desire to deal mercifully with their patients may lead them to break the law, for the best of reasons.

The complexity of the issues we have discussed in this chapter is testimony to the moral seriousness of the human imagination, not its corruption. It is because we are creatures blessed and afflicted with consciousness that we find ourselves in these predicaments. The fact that, for most of us, there are no simple solutions to these problems should not dismay us. Our awareness of complexity is due to the sweep of our vision, and the fact that we are more often confronted with opposing goods than with simple choices between good and evil. These conflicts are our tragedy, but they are also our glory, so we should think very carefully before exchanging them for any theory of human nature that removes the pain of conflict by excising human freedom. This is the perennial attraction of those total systems that continue to appear in human history. Those who follow them have the reward of absolute moral certainty as they confront life's choices, but the price they pay is the need to force the breadth of humanity onto the narrow template of their own imagination. To change the metaphor, they want humanity to march to the sound of a single drummer. Fortunately, there are always plenty of people around who prefer ethical jazz and its skilled improvisations, because they believe it is a truer expression of the real human condition.

CHAPTER SIX

The Reproductive Supermarket

Bertrand Russell once remarked that zeal was a bad mark for a cause. No one is zealous about the two times table. We are zealous about issues over which there is disagreement and about which there can be no absolute certainty because there is no one to provide it. In this book we have been demonstrating that claim by our exploration of a number of complex ethical issues which decent-minded people are in disagreement about. Most of the things about which we dispute are never permanently settled, because not everyone is prepared to accept the authority of the various infallible schemes that are on offer. Uncertainty makes us anxious and anxiety tempts us to resolve complex issues by simple solutions. This anxiety is particularly pronounced in the debate in the field of bio-ethics, where we are confronted with complex issues provoked by the new reproductive technologies and by advances in the science and technology of genetics.

The first thing to note here is that some of these techniques have been around for many years. In 1766 John Hunter advised a linen draper suffering from a congenital condition called hypospadias to use a warm syringe to introduce his semen into his wife. However, this first successful use of artificial insemination by a husband (AIH) was not reported by Hunter, because of the social and religious attitudes of the time.[1] In 1897 the controversy caused by physicians practising assisted insemination led to its formal condemnation by the Roman Catholic Church. It is worth pausing for a few moments here to reflect upon these religious anxieties over what is now thought to be a process that is morally unproblematic, AIH. The use of donor sperm is obviously difficult for people within moral communities that believe sexual acts should only occur within the marriage relationship. The Vatican's instruction on the matter forbids all forms of non-coital technology, because they separate the act of intercourse from the possibility of procreation and involve masturbation and third parties in the utilisation of semen. According to many traditional religions, including Roman Catholicism, donor insemination is compared to adultery, infidelity or rape and is, therefore, held to be morally repugnant. However, in Islam and Judaism the principle on which the objection is based differs from the Roman Catholic objection. Both Islam and Judaism base their objections on the loss of identifiable lineage and the danger of incestuous marriage.[2] In the Roman Catholic tradition the objection is not only to the adulterous element introduced by the third party, but to the masturbation that is the usual prelude to the act of artificial insemination. Here the ingenuity of traditional casuistry takes over, and tries to find ways to help married couples. Within the traditional moral perspective, mastur-bation is wrong, because it is a sexual act that is not open to the possibility of procreation, even though it may be hard for us to understand why, in this context, it cannot be seen as an act that is precisely intended to achieve conception. Nevertheless, the Catholic moral tradition is more flexible than it often appears, and it offers a number of methods, however cumbersome, that try to get round the problem. The most obvious is for the husband and wife to have sexual intercourse and for the semen to be retrieved from the woman afterwards, usually by a process of aspiration. Another permitted approach is by the use of the canonical condom, a pre-perforated, non-spermicidal French Letter, worn by the husband during intercourse, placed immediately in a container after withdrawal and express-delivered to the clinic where it is stored until the insemination procedure is carried out. We may think all these elaborate, casuistical devices cast an unattractive spotlight upon some of the more inflexible aspects of religious ethics, but they also show that even very traditional religious systems do try to adapt their principles to changing circumstances. We have already thought about the incommensurability of different moral systems and the need to create space enough for them to live together. Traditional religions find the new assisted reproduction technologies difficult, so we should, perhaps, salute them when they try to stretch their principles to fit the new discoveries. It probably ought to be added at this point, however, before we continue our exploration of artificial insemination, which is the most basic and elementary of the new techniques, that lay members of the religious traditions in question seem to suffer little anxiety in adapting to the new technologies. The ethical issues will become more complex and taxing as we move further into this field, but few people nowadays spend much time worrying about the moral status of masturbation. One clinician said to me that 98% of men masturbate, and the other 2% are liars.

Most people would see no moral difficulty in AIH, no matter how the sperm was retrieved, but artificial insemination by a donor (AID) is more morally problematic. Even people who do not rule it out on *a priori* religious grounds have to go through some kind of ethical calculus in deciding about it. Let me briefly suggest what the problems are. The intrusion of a third party into the relationship is the basis of the moral problematic. Since we are now accustomed to blood transfusions and organ donations, however, the involvement of third parties is something we accept and even celebrate as evidence of human altruism. However, the anonymity of the donor creates particular difficulties. At the moment, the Act that governs these matters in Britain insists on the anonymity of the sperm donor. There is probably a pragmatic ground to this protection, based on the fear that men would stop donating sperm if they thought that in years to come their donor offspring might start queuing at their doorstep.

Another aspect of donor insemination that troubles people is the payment of donors. In this country, most donors seem to be students and the small sum of money they receive for each sperm donation, about £15 a shot, is what seems to motivate them to become sperm donors in the first place. Many people are made uneasy by this commercial element in the transaction and would like to move to a culture in which sperm donors act altruistically. Intriguingly, women who donate eggs tend to do it for altruistic reasons. Donating eggs can be painful and risky, but women do it out of altruism. Donating sperm is mildly pleasurable, but men seem to want to be paid for it. Female readers may not be surprised by that melancholy contrast. Clinicians, though they agree that a culture of altruism is better than a commercial culture, are worried that if payment is banned the number of donors will radically decrease and make it almost impossible to offer the service.

A more profound moral difficulty for people is created by the effect that knowledge of their origins might have upon donor offspring. Unfortunately, since an air of secrecy still cloaks the whole field of assisted reproduction, many children are not informed about their origins in ways that help them come to terms with them. The best practice seems to be for knowledge of their origins to be an unproblematic part of the children's consciousness from an early age, thereby removing the trauma of shock and discovery when the disclosure is finally made. As a matter of fact, surveys seem to show that donor offspring do very well in life, because they find themselves in families, of whatever shape, that want them and offer them the kind of security that only love can give to children. The paradox of these lives is that the ability to question and reflect upon their origins is itself a consequence of the gifted nature of their beginnings.

It may be, however, that the need for sperm donation will soon be a thing of the past. There is a comparatively new technique called intracytoplasmic sperm injection, or ICSI, which offers the possibility of biological fatherhood to almost all men with types of infertility that were previously thought to be incurable. In crude layman's terms, male infertility seems to be caused by the comparative lack of spermatozoa or by the unathletic nature of the sperm that are produced. The new technique overcomes these handicaps by injecting a sperm under the outer zone of the egg, thus giving it a head start in the process of fertilisation. Every new technique has risks, and people are asking if it is wise for us to assist feeble sperm that could not make it on their own. Maybe nature had a reason for making it difficult. Maybe we are storing up problems for the future. There are some concerned voices speaking out, but most opinion in the profession is confident that the procedure is safe and offers the opportunity of fatherhood to men for whom it would have been impossible a few years ago. Traditional religious groups, provided sperm is retrieved in ways they approve, are likely to view this technique as being morally unproblematic. The irony is, of course, that it was developed and made possible by methods of experimentation that the religious groups in question would have repudiated. But let us now move deeper into the moral problematic itself, and consider the implications of some of the more controversial techniques.

The approach that governs my own thinking about these matters would not be accepted by everyone. We have observed throughout this book that we live in a society that is characterised by pluralism in its value systems. How does an ethically plural society, which encloses many different value systems, make decisions in sensitive areas that require legislation? Is there an approach we can adopt that might enable us to regulate complex issues without imposing our values upon other people? Behind our attitude to these matters there usually lies an implicit or explicit philosophy of nature. The most extreme view sees nature as a fixed and unalterable reality that must not be tampered with. There is a certain passive logic in this position, but it precludes all human advances in knowledge and is rarely followed in its purity. A second position permits intervention in the processes of nature to heal or enhance existing human life, but it places a veto on all procedures that would artificially interfere with the creation of life itself. It would permit heart surgery, organ transplantation and other interventionist medical techniques, but it would ring-fence the reproductive area. In our discussion of artificial insemination we noted the constraining effect of this ethic upon the most straightforward of the assisted reproduction techniques. We would expect the restraints to become more rigorous as the processes become more complex and, therefore, morally more problematic. We'll look at some of these difficult areas later in this chapter.

The third attitude to these matters, the one in which I find myself, recognises that the human is by nature an intervening and developmental reality. It is natural for humanity to intervene, so the paradox is that what we do, though it may appear to be contrary to nature, is in fulfilment of our own nature. All of these new discoveries are the result of the application of human consciousness to the universe itself. For the first time since we emerged from the chemical soup that gave us being, we are able to understand how we came to be in the first place. Our human history has been an evolution towards that under-standing and the new freedoms (as well as their correspond-ing dangers) that it has brought us. The new genetics is yet another extension of the role of consciousness and human understanding over what was previously blind chance. Every extension of human freedom brings anxiety and danger and calls for careful debate, but the advances of science call for celebration and caution rather than denun-ciation and rejection. This seems to be consistent with the evolutionary paradigm that sees creation as a dynamic, evolving reality. This means, however, that since we cannot rule out developments on *a priori* grounds, each situation has to be dealt with on its own merits, governed by the principle that life itself is a good and sacred thing and that we should not harm it intentionally. We remember how many of the advances in science and the treatment of disease have been made against the tide of opinion. (For instance, when chloroform was discovered, it was objected to on the grounds that it was unnatural to anaesthetise pain and that nature intended us to feel it.) Nevertheless, a proper caution is appropriate in these matters, as well as a desire not to quench too quickly the spirit of enquiry that is characteristic of our species. Britain has moved firmly but cautiously in these areas. It has decided to regulate rather than outlaw the new technologies. While recognising that for some sections of the moral community these technologies are repugnant, we have sought, on the basis of a balanced judgement, to regulate rather than outlaw them and, in so doing, protect those who would make use of them. Let me sketch in something of the historical background.

In 1978, Lesley and John Brown of Oldham in Lancashire gave birth to the first child conceived in a test tube or glass dish, *in vitro*, in Latin. R.G. Edwards and Patrick Steptoe, the doctors who performed the first successful *in vitro* fertilisation (IVF) removed a single egg from Lesley Brown's ovary and placed it in a dish. John Brown's sperm was added to the dish and fertilisation occurred. After waiting for the fertilised egg to divide three times, the doctors placed it in Lesley Brown's uterus. The birth of Louise Brown shocked and excited the public. In response to increasing public concern, the Government set up a Committee of Enquiry in 1982, chaired by Mary Warnock, now Baroness Warnock. The prime function of the Warnock Committee was to consider what policies and safeguards should be adopted for IVF and embryo research. The Committee published its findings in 1984. The Warnock Report was debated extensively in Parliament and there was much public consultation. Opinions on the Report were sought from all sides – moral, religious, legal, social. The debate was hot. Then the Government started to frame its proposals for legislation.

In 1987 the Government published a White Paper that contained alternative proposals on the morally problematic area of embryo research, which were to be decided by a free vote in Parliament. It was proposed that embryo research should either be banned completely, or that it should be permitted subject to strict controls. These controls would include an outright ban on contentious issues, such as cloning and creation of hybrids, and the regulation of research by a new statutory body set up to license and invigilate upon the new reproductive technologies, the Human Fertilisation and Embryology Authority (HFEA). Debates on the White Paper were held in both Houses early in 1988. The Human Fertilisation and Embryology Bill became an Act of Parliament in November 1990. So, in the UK infertility clinics and embryo research centres are now regulated through legislation. And the regulation is done by the HFEA through its licensing system. I'd like now to touch on some of the ethical and social issues which are involved in infertility treatment and embryo research.

When Parliament considered the legislation, research on human embryos was the most emotive of all the issues involved. When clinicians treat women with IVF they create several embryos. Using various processes, they stimulate the woman's ovaries and harvest her eggs. They add her partner's sperm to the eggs, thereby creating multiple embryos. To avoid multiple births, however, no more than three embryos, the ones most likely to succeed, are put back. The other embryos are frozen and stored for use in future treatment cycles, if necessary. These embryos may not be stored for more than ten years, and they cannot be used without the written consent of both partners. Sometimes unwanted embryos are donated to other women, sometimes they are offered for research. For many people, this research is morally problematic. While all this was being debated in Britain, some people thought that any kind of research, at any time, on living creatures – especially human ones – was morally wrong. To them the stage at which living cells actually become human was irrelevant: the fundamental issue was that from the moment of fertilisation a unique life was being created, whether by normal or by artificial means. They argued that, since one would never carry out experimentation on an adult without consent, the same rule should apply to embryos, which are incapable of consent. We considered the force and logic of this approach when we thought about abortion. We noted then that, even when the embryo was held to have full human moral status (the status of personhood) certain inconsistencies emerged, but that the attraction of the position was its clarity and the fact that it removed the anguish of the kind that characterised other approaches.

To those who believe that the immature embryo is just a bunch of cells or a bundle of tissue, the moral argument against embryo research is exotic. However, people who accord the embryo some moral status, though not full personhood, are likely to feel a level of moral discomfort about embryo research that requires them to balance different goods against each other. The main argument is the potential benefits of embryo research. Success rates with IVF, it was argued at the time, would be improved as a result of experimentation, thus bettering the condition of those suffering from infertility; there would be better understanding of unexplained infertility and the heartbreak of repeated miscarriages; and newer contraceptive techniques could be developed. But the greatest potential benefit was the ability to diagnose and treat genetic abnormality before the embryo was implanted. Approximately 14,000 infants, or 2% of all babies, are born each year with a genetic defect, a topic we'll return to.

When the free vote on embryo research was taken, Parliament decided to allow it to continue within a strict framework of statutory controls. In reaching this conclusion, Parliament resolved a major ethical question that had been debated for years, though not to everyone's satisfaction. As we saw in the case of abortion, those who oppose embryo research on intrinsic moral grounds are unimpressed by votes in parliament, so it continues to be a highly vexed question. As the law stands at the moment, however, research on embryos is permitted up to the time of the emergence of the primitive or neural streak at fourteen days.

Before taking a longer look at the ethical dilemmas created for us by recent advances in gene science, let me go back to the ethics of donation for a moment. The Human Fertilisation and Embryology Authority is under a statutory requirement to keep a formal register of information about the treatment of individual patients, the use made of all sperm or eggs provided by donors and any children born as a result. This register has a dual purpose. It is obviously a method of monitoring the work of treatment and research centres, but it has a more controversial use, which has turned previous practice on its head. The Act permits people over 18 to have access to information about their genetic background – important if there is a chance that they might be related to someone they want to marry. As we have already seen, the Act protects donor anonymity. The Government's attitude is that there should be a period of further consultation before the anonymity issue is resolved. Some think that donor offspring should have full rights to information about their genetic history, while others think that the anonymity of donors should be protected. Some clinicians fear that disclosure would inhibit donors from volunteering. There is a parallel with the history of the adoption laws. Before the 1975 Children Act, parents gave up children for adoption secure in the knowledge that they would remain anonymous. After 1975, the law permitted children of 18 to obtain the names of their genetic parents. Research has shown that this change benefited adopted children, though it caused unforeseen distress when the legislation took effect. There is a significant difference in the case of donors. The 1990 Act expressly states it will not act retrospectively to reveal the name of the donor. Let me turn back now to a number of vexing ethical issues.

As long as artificial reproductive techniques involved only the mixing of eggs and sperm outside the body and their subsequent implantation in the woman, the moral problematic was not too difficult to deal with. With the daily acceleration of knowledge in the science of genes and the possibilities of gene therapy, we are moving into a more contentious realm. Let me sketch in something of the background before giving examples of the new developments.

We all know that the body is made up of many different cells that perform different tasks. Genes instruct the cells on how they should operate, in order to carry out their allotted tasks. Although almost all cells contain a full set of genes, only those that are appropriate to a particular type of cell and the functions it must perform are actually switched on. Genes provide the instructions for our development from a fertilised egg to a fully grown adult. They continue throughout our lives to provide the information necessary for the maintenance and functioning of our bodies. Genes are sections of DNA (deoxyribonucleic acid) that are contained in the chromosomes that were passed on from our parents

at conception. Pembrey offers a useful analogy to explain the relationship between genes, DNA and chromosomes. He compares a chromosome to an audio cassette, with DNA to the tape inside and genes to the songs on the tape. Genes are not separate from DNA, they are a part of it in the same way that a song is an integral part of the tape.[3]

New methods for isolating, identifying and storing genes are being accompanied by numerous techniques designed to manipulate and transform them. The most revolutionary of the techniques is called recombinant DNA, which takes two unrelated organisms that could not mate in nature, isolating a piece of DNA from each, and then recombining the two pieces of genetic material. Recombinant DNA has been called a kind of biological sewing machine that can stitch together the genetic fabric of unrelated organisms.[4] Some analysts believe that this feat rivals the importance of harnessing fire in its significance for human history. Here are some examples of its application. In 1984 scientists in England fused together embryo cells from a goat and a sheep and placed the fused embryo into a surrogate animal, which gave birth to a sheep-goat chimera, the first example of the blending of two completely unrelated animal species in history. In 1986 scientists took the gene whose product emits light in fireflies and inserted it into the genetic code of a tobacco plant. The tobacco leaves glow.[5] The first commercially grown gene-spliced food crops were planted in 1996, genetically engineered to kill insects. Much research in animal husbandry occurs in the new field of *pharming*. Researchers are transforming herds and flocks into bio-factories to produce pharmaceutical products, medicines and nutrients. The new *pharming* technology moved a step closer to reality on 22 February 1997, when Ian Wilmut, an embryologist in Scotland, announced the cloning of the first

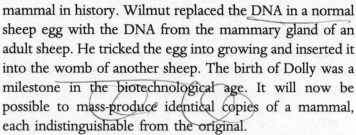

mammal in history. Wilmut replaced the DNA in a normal sheep egg with the DNA from the mammary gland of an adult sheep. He tricked the egg into growing and inserted it into the womb of another sheep. The birth of Dolly was a milestone in the biotechnological age. It will now be possible to mass-produce identical copies of a mammal, each indistinguishable from the original.

The medical applications of biotechnology are enormous. For example, skin replacement on burn victims is notoriously difficult and heart-breakingly slow. Hospitals are now using artificial skin, cultured and grown in the laboratory, to treat serious burn victims. One company in Boston boasts that it can take a few cells from a human foreskin and manufacture from it four acres of skin. It is claimed that engineered structured tissue will replace plastic and metal prostheses for bones and joints in the next century. And scientists hope to be able to isolate and identify the gene or genes responsible for the more than four thousand genetic diseases that afflict human beings. Before returning to the subject of genetic disease and the ethical challenge its treatment creates, let me go back to Dolly and the debate she initiated.

Cloning is the creating of genetically identical individuals. Until recently, it was thought that cloning was prohibited by the Human Fertilisation and Embryology Act of 1990. Even before Dolly came along, however, there was a type of cloning, involving splitting the embryo, which was not prohibited absolutely. In theory, the benefit of splitting an embryo would be to a woman undergoing IVF treatment who had produced only one embryo. Splitting the embryo would give more embryos for treatment and improve her chances of pregnancy. There has been no published research on the viability of the technique anywhere in the world, but it could be developed. In law, it could be allowed under a licence from the Authority. The HFEA decided, however, that it would not allow cloning in treatment for infertility nor for research directed towards the development of cloning for such treatment. Its reasons included:

- people's instinctive reaction against creating genetically identical individuals
- cloning may be considered socially undesirable because it may be thought to dilute individuality
- cloning raises fears of eugenics and attempts to reproduce embryos for particular characteristics, the so-called 'designer baby'
- embryos could be put back in a woman at different times so that she would have identical children of different ages, with potentially disturbing implications for the children themselves.

The cloning controversy was a good example of the kind of moral panic that can engulf a society when faced with new developments in science. Pictures were painted of a genetic apocalypse in which the world would be peopled with multiple copies of the same person. It was predicted that wealthy narcissists could achieve immortality by simply cloning themselves over and over again. Even if that nightmare were to happen, it is worth remembering that each clone, or twin, to use less threatening parlance, would be a unique individual with a unique history, so there is no way the same person could be multiplied. Identical twins, which is what we are talking about, are separate individuals. Individuality is much more than genes, so we should brace ourselves against moral panic and make our calculations with cool heads. I personally can see no strong moral objection to the kind of embryo splitting that would enable a woman with a single embryo to maximise her chances of conception. I would have more difficulty with the idea of identical twins of different ages, though I suspect my response here is caused by instinctive reaction rather than a thought-out point of view.

Cloning is upsetting, but something that is just as emotionally challenging (when we confront the issue for the first time) is the possibility of creating embryos and, where we know there is risk in the family of genetic disease, testing them by a process called pre-implantation diagnosis, and replacing only those embryos that are free of the disorder. The technique is in the early stages of development but it raises some interesting ethical challenges. Some people object to pre-implantation and pre-natal screening, not because of their views on the moral status of the embryo or fetus, but because they believe it is an affront to existing people with disabilities. Pre-implantation diagnosis is premised upon the discarding of embryos that are diseased, and pre-natal diagnosis is usually, though not always, the prelude to the abortion of a fetus that would be disabled if born. Disabled people see these new technologies as posing a question against their own existence. It has been argued that there is no inconsistency in treating the disabled with respect and doing everything to integrate them into society, and at the same time preferring the birth of normal children to handicapped children. We can retain a preference for the birth of children without disability, while at the same time trying to make sure this preference does not become discrimination against disabled people. Those who campaign for the rights of the disabled will tell us that disability is socially constructed and that most disability could be overcome with proper support. Another challenge that is likely to face us in the near future is the request by a disabled couple, such as a profoundly deaf man and woman, to utilise the new technology to produce disabled offspring, intentionally designed to fit their parents' culture and community of the disabled. This is another example of the way in which ethics often confronts us with choices between competing goods rather than between an obvious good and an obvious evil. Personally, I am troubled by the effect of the new technologies, not only upon disabled people, but upon our whole attitude towards the different or the technically imperfect. Nevertheless, I would not be prepared to dictate my choices to people caught in these dilemmas. At the same time, I believe it is important to celebrate and not simply tolerate the differences between the capacities of human beings, and to recognise that the less fortunate in life are frequently the keepers of values the rest of society would be poorer without.

Surrogate motherhood is another issue that obsesses the more unrestrained sections of the press. Let me try to summarise the arguments for and against it. If we argue that it is every couple's natural right to become parents, or every woman's right to bear a child, surrogacy can be advocated as the only means available for some couples to have a child biologically related to one or both of them. It can be seen as a supreme act of generosity for a woman to bear a child for another. And various instances where sisters, mothers and daughters, have done just that, might be cited to justify this claim.

Those disturbed by it see it as an attack on traditional values, not least marriage itself. They claim that an experience that should be confined to a loving relationship between two people is devalued and distorted by the intrusion of a third party – and not an anonymous third party, as with a semen donor, but a person whose involvement would be far greater for far longer. By supplanting the female partner, there is a risk that the surrogate mother will change her mind, something that has often happened in a blaze of publicity, and decide to keep the child herself. It is also argued that surrogacy damages the relationship between the child and the intended mother, because the natural bonds will be with the surrogate mother. Finally, it is said that it is degrading for a woman to hire out her uterus for financial gain, and for a child to have been born via a financial transaction.

'Wombs for rent' was a typical tabloid comment on the controversy. In 1985 the Surrogacy Arrangements Act was passed in Britain. It banned commercial surrogacy and made it illegal to advertise for surrogates. It created an important distinction between the law in Britain and the law in the United States. In the United States, commercial surrogacy is legal; people can *own* embryos; and disputed claims of ownership cause distress. In Britain, nobody has the right to own an embryo, just as nobody can own any other person.

Let me draw this chapter to some sort of conclusion. In this book I have tried to follow a middle way as an example of the wisest way to proceed in the field of human values. This is something like a general application of Aristotle's doctrine of virtue as a mean between two extremes. This middle way, though it lays one open to attacks from two sides, has a lot to be said for it. Another reality we have been acknowledging is the fact of moral pluralism, the fact that we exist in a culture with different, often competing, moral traditions. A third implicit assumption behind my approach has been the dynamic nature of humanity. I like the metaphor of the automobile, wisely equipped with brakes and accelerator. The purpose of the car is movement, but to drive safely it is important to be able to slow down and stop, sometimes suddenly. Inevitably, you get drivers who crawl, drivers who speed and drivers who prefer to keep their car up on blocks in the garage where it will come to no harm. I have argued that we are born to motor, but that we should do it carefully. We are confronted with unique challenges today, some of which I have sketched in this chapter. Genetic engineering is the ultimate human tool. It can be put to good or bad uses. Knowing something about the human tendency to abuse knowledge, we'll try to handle it circumspectly, for the bettering of ourselves and the planet we inhabit. Like all wise motorists, we'll keep moving, but we'll make sure our brakes are in working order.

Deciding for Ourselves

It would be difficult to exaggerate the moral confusions of our day and the urgency and importance of finding an agreed basis for our conduct towards one another as sharers of life on this planet. Various elements, all of them related, have brought us to where we are today, but the main and enduring one is our own passion for knowledge. In us the universe has started thinking about itself, and in our own era knowledge of the universe and of our place in it has increased at an alarming but exhilarating rate. Modern science has been characterised by two apparently contradictory tendencies. It has increasingly understood the nature of the big picture of the expanding universe, and the new physics has opened our minds to the unimaginable vastness of it all. The glorious paradox at the centre of it is our own consciousness, so that, after fifteen billion years, a tiny, fragile part of the universe knows not only much about how it all came to be, but how it goes on working. The counterpoint to this big picture is the submicroscopic work of the science of genetics which shows us, in tiny detail, how we humans have come to be what we are. For most of our history we have been at the mercy of forces we did not understand, which were coded into our own bodies. We are now poised on the brink of having the freedom to shape the very genes that previously shaped us. We are no longer constrained by our evolutionary origins. We shall soon possess the dangerous freedom to shape our own future and the kind of society we want. It is this potentiality that is most frightening to people who are committed, for whatever reasons, to a fixed understanding of human nature and its possibilities.

The extraordinary discoveries of science have been the main story of our time, but there has been another that has been just as important. We have applied the same passion for knowledge and understanding to the history of our own moral, religious and political systems, so that we are now in the precarious position of watching ourselves in action, like someone on the high trapeze who is suddenly overwhelmed with self-consciousness when he should be out of his own head and operating on instinct and intuition. It is precisely our consciousness of ourselves and our history that makes our situation so frightening and so interesting. I have claimed in this book that we now understand that most moral systems reflected and gave support to external structures of authority, because until very recent times most human systems were systems of command: domination systems, based on an ethic of obedience to authority. Obeying is what people did. There were always human ways to modify or soften the system, but they only proved the rule that society was a finely articulated command system in which we all knew our place and the places of those above and below us, and we took it all for granted. The system was protected by the claims of revelation and tradition: it came from God, so it was beyond human questioning; it was the way things had always been. And it was handed on in a way that potently interiorised it in the human psyche. To challenge it was perilous and isolating, but the very weight of its prestige made it difficult to challenge. How could the individual raise her tiny protest effectively against something so venerable and so authoritative? I was reminded of how difficult it has always been to challenge authority when I last visited St Peter's in Rome. I was there with a few friends to make radio programmes for the BBC. One of the party, who was guiding us, was a Catholic priest and scholar whose relationship with the great Roman Church was one of fiercely critical loyalty, with the emphasis on the critical. I was overwhelmed by St Peter's and was made to feel puny and irrelevant in its confident vastness. I told John how I felt, how I almost wanted to hold up my hands in surrender and submission, saying, 'OK, I give up, take me in.' 'That's what the bastards want you to do,' John replied, throwing a look of exasperated affection back over St Peter's Square.

The great traditions all had their casualties, of course, but we learned to accept them as the price we paid for continuity and stability. Women and children were probably the ones who paid the highest price, since they have always been the ones who were most vulnerable to the abusive power of the systems that enclosed them. Gradually, during the twentieth century, the great traditions started to erode, and the process of disintegration has now reached a critical stage. Various factors have contributed to this process of disintegration. The one major factor I will not attempt to assess is the corruption of the systems themselves, and the revulsion they often created in good people. The carnage of the Great War undermined our confidence in the wisdom and competence of the great institutions of the state. The complacency and inertia of the churches undermined our sense that they were genuine representatives of God on earth. So the inner corruption of the grand traditions was a major factor in the creation of the contemporary malaise, but the most potent factor was our own questioning rationality. Our passion for knowledge has led us to ask questions and to dig for the truth beneath the official answers we are given, so that we can confront the underlying narratives that really account for what has gone on, and not the official versions. We began to question the authority of authority itself, and its narrative of divine origin. We have also noted how important the anarchic power of the market economy has been in the erosion of tradition, with its contempt for boundaries and its creation of new systems of power. One of the most potent elements in this mix has been the liberalising of the status of women and young people in our culture, the very elements who were most at risk from, as well as being most protected by, the previous command systems. The strongest factor in the current situation, however, is probably the rejection of authority, as such, in its extrinsic guise, as something imposed that expects obedience. That type of consciousness is still around in the remnants of traditional institutions, not least in some of the churches, and there is much nostalgia for its hey day, but it is no longer a part of the consciousness of most people under the age of forty today.

An examination of the state of marriage today provides a good example of the effect of this process. Marriage is one of the traditional institutions that claims to be of specific divine origin, though we have already noted that the Bible, in particular, seems to know a profusion of family structures. Marriage went through many phases until it coalesced in our own time into what became known as the nuclear family, consisting of a husband, wife, and two or three children. During its flourishing phase, the undoubted success of this institution as a way of protecting and nurturing children was based on a clearly articulated system of roles, with the husband as bread-winner and authority figure, and the wife as nurturer and home-maker. The cement that bound the structure together was the notion of marital indissolubility, whether as a religious or social constraint. It is easy both to romanticise and to caricature this tradition, to see it as an idyll of ideal human relationships or as the perfect arena for abuse and torment. Most families probably contained elements of both, but there is no doubt that traditional marriage had terrible casualties. We have known for a long time the price women often had to pay for their protected status; in our own day we are beginning to realise that behind the suburban curtains of the ideal family there has existed, in many places, a nightmare of abuse of children and the enduring heartache it caused.

But whether we mourn or celebrate its demise, marriage is no longer the institution it was. People still get married, of course, and will probably continue to do so, but it is no longer an impermeable institution that protects and hides the lives that are lived within it. The curtains have been opened, and so have the doors. Women no longer define themselves in the way that cemented the traditional marriage. Very few people today defend the tradition of marriage in the traditional way. When they commend it now they commend it in untraditional ways, and people who get married or stay married do it with untraditional expectations. Marriage is now about personal relationships, about emotional intimacy, about reciprocity. And there is always a clause in invisible print at the bottom of the contract that says the relationship will not be endured if it becomes abusive or deeply unsatisfying. Marriage has now become provisional, something from which there is a clearly marked exit. That means it is no longer marriage in the traditional sense at all. We have already noticed that intelligent institutions adapt in this way if they want to survive. Marriage will probably survive and it will probably go on adapting to new circumstances, but it is no longer the only structure available to us for nurturing or expressing our relationships. Today there is a whole repertoire of relational forms in modern society, and for young people there is a new, floating family network called friendship that seems to provide one of the few permanent elements in their lives.

It should go without saying that there is loss as well as gain in this new reality. The human predicament is always prone to pain, loneliness and discontent. The old traditional way of doing things provided security, as well as opportunities for abuse and contempt. That is why we are always tempted to look back at and mourn the places we have left behind, though we probably did not feel particularly terrific about them when we there at the time. That, too, is part of our intrinsic discontent, and it is here that memory plays its most painful games with us. But we cannot go back, in spite of our nostalgia for the past and the siren voices that pretend we can choose to live there again if we want to. The past is gone from us, with all its pain and joy, with all its goodness and badness. We can't go back to the past, but we might be able to influence the future by taking a look at the present. The traditions that no longer work for us were ones we built ourselves, so the chances are that we can build new ones for the future. They will probably be less solid than the ones from the past, more makeshift and provisional, but that will suit our day and our needs.

The main characteristic of our new, lightweight moral tradition will be the principle of consent. Just as obedience to the commands of authority, whether God, state or any other centre of power, was the dominant characteristic of ancient traditions, so, today, is the consent of our reason and emotion. Today, we expect to be persuaded by coherent argument and the consequential results of particular policies. In the drugs debate, for instance, we are no longer prepared to accept the claims of government and other related institutions that the human use of drugs has to be fought against like an enemy. We make distinctions between different substances and their effects. We even believe there are better ways to tackle the tragedies of addiction to hard drugs than by making desperate criminals out of the unfortunate people whose lives have already been ruined by abuse of substances that most people manage to use without descending into the abyss. We can even point to better ways of helping addicts than the official systems on offer in this country. And we do not, in any case, believe that the war on drugs can be won, even if we think we know what winning it would look like. We may not ourselves have the best recipe, but we would like to encourage a rational discussion of the subject that treated it as just another problem, and not some mystical evil that has invaded us from another realm and has to be fought with bell, book, candle and accompanying mantra.

We know that as human animals we have a tendency to excess, to the abuse of good things, such as food, drugs and sex. There is something in our late capitalist culture that lends an extra weight to this tendency. For most of our history, most human beings spent their lives working hard just in order to survive. The opportunities for excess and addiction did not exist for the vast bulk of humanity. The tiny elite at the top of the social pyramid were prone to the sins of excess, but they were thought to be a diseased minority, exceptions to the human norm. In today's societies of abundance and choice we are all tempted to neurotic excess, and we know it. That is why the book shops are overflowing with publications on lifestyle and values, telling us how to conquer our tendency to self-destruction and unhappiness. Some of the books on offer invite us to enter a total system of one sort or another. Total systems continue to assure us that only by handing over our nature and its joys and miseries to them will we find peace. And there is certainly a peace of sorts to be found by committing ourselves to an absolute system. It will only work, of course, if we can persuade ourselves that we believe it. Some people try it for a time, till the violence it does to other values they cherish makes it impossible to carry on. They may be confused and saddened by their experience of the sexual merry-go-round of today, and leap off it into some system, probably religious, that tells people exactly who may sleep with whom, and who may never sleep with anyone. If they have gay and lesbian friends they will find that most of the total systems, especially some of the Christian ones, refuse them any possibility of sexual pleasure, in the name of an abstract principle that is usually associated with one of those divine commands we have noticed throughout this book. It is at this point that there often arises one of those important moral conflicts in the breast of the believer who knows that the system that has been adopted runs counter to some of her own deepest values. She experiences great personal dissonance, as her own sense of loyalty to her gay and lesbian friends, and their human status, struggles with the confident authoritarianism of the adopted system. Her decision can go either way, but I would hope it would go against the arrogance of the official systems that lack the imaginative capacity to embrace humanity in all its profuse variety.

By abandoning absolute systems we have not, however, solved the problem of how best to deal with the complexities of sexuality. If we cannot argue ourselves into one of the systems that apply a strict rules morality, we will find ourselves trying to respond to situations with grace appropriate to the event. It is here that the old Greek idea about virtue might be helpful. It acknowledges that we ought to delight in the pleasures of the table and of the bed, but it also knows that our tendency to excess can lead us and those closest to us into unhappiness and pain, so it counsels moderation, the discovery of the mean that usually lies between two extremes. This is why those who try to follow the ethic of moderation are likely to be depressed by the excesses of the shagging culture in the youth scene today. Of course, that culture of excess is absolutely consistent with the lack of balance that often characterises the young, and it will probably do them little lasting damage, though there will, inevitably, be casualties. One of the most difficult conversations to initiate is the one between the generations about drugs and sex. As long as the conversation is conducted from the commanding heights of morality on the part of the older generation towards the younger, it will be heard, but ignored. If we could initiate a discussion on the possibility of an ethic of sexuality that was based on the value of moderation as well as the goodness of pleasure, we might be able to develop a new morality of consent.

One of the most important balances to achieve in the new morality of consent would be between celebrating an allowable diversity in ethical approaches and refusing to accept the claim that no system is better than any other. We have acknowledged the importance of relativism in moral systems. We have recognised that moral struggles are frequently between competing goods, rather than between a straight good and a straight evil. But that does not mean that anything goes, that there are no forms of conduct which, as rational human beings, we should condemn. The principle of harm is a very broad one, and it calls for subtle elucidations in particular situations, but it is a useful guide in steering our way through the currents of debate about what is or is not allowable or moral behaviour. We might be persuaded to allow a variety of approaches to the use of drugs. We might be prepared to affirm that there are many sexualities, and that people should be allowed to express themselves consensually in private as they want to. There would be limits, however, that any civilised society would want to impose. We would expect consent to be an important element in the sexual equation, so that would rule out forcing unwanted sexual attentions on others; and it would warn us against exploiting any power relationship over another for sexual purposes. The principle of harm would also rule out the gross and obvious assaults of violence and murder that continue to characterise human society. But the main characteristic of our time will continue to be its prodigal variety and competitiveness. We are enormously creative creatures, because our adventurousness and appetite for knowledge is insatiable. This is what creates endless and fascinating difficulties for us, some of which I have rehearsed in this book; but that is also our glory, it is what makes us human, and we should rejoice in it.

Notes

Chapter 1

1. Friedrich Nietzsche, *On the Genealogy of Morals*, Second Essay: section 16ff, Oxford University Press, 1996.
2. Fulke Greville, Lord Brooke, *Chorus Sacerdotum*.
3. Alasdair MacIntyre, *After Virtue*, University of Notre Dame Press, 1981, pp.105ff.

Chapter 2

1. Arthur Schopenhauer, *The World as Will and as Representation*, vol. 2, Dover Publications, NY, 1966, p.532.
2. Ibid, p.538.
3. Ibid, p.540.
4. Ibid, p.551.
5. Ibid, p.556.
6. Michel Foucault, *The Use of Pleasure*, Penguin Books, 1992, p.50ff.
7. Lawrence Osborne, *The Poisoned Embrace*, Vintage, 1994, p. 68ff.
8. Foucault, *The Use of Pleasure*, p.116.
9. Osborne, *The Poisoned Embrace*, p.10.
10. Matthew Fox, *Original Blessing*, Bear and Company, Santa Fe, 1983.
11. Osborne, *The Poisoned Embrace*, pp.13–14.
12. Given personally to the author by a young disc jockey.
13. John Harris, *Wonderwoman and Superman*, Oxford University Press, 1992, p.42.

Chapter 3

1. Pat Barker, *Regeneration*, Viking, 1991.
2. Wilfrid Owen, *Collected Poems*, Chatto and Windus, 1963, p.31.

3. Harris, *Wonderwoman and Superman*, Oxford University Press, 1992, p. 42.
4. Nietzsche, *The Anti-Christ*, Penguin, 1990, section 26, p. 150.
5. Stuart Blanch, quoted in John Goldingay: *Theological Diversity and the Authority of the Old Testament*, Paternoster Press, 1995.

Chapter 4

1. Anthony Giddens, *Beyond Left and Right*, Polity Press, 1996, p.6.
2. 'Cannabis in California', in *The New York Times*, 20 July 1997.
3. Danny Kushlick, 'The Campaign against Drugs', in *The Guardian*, 1 November 1997.
4. Ibid.

Chapter 5

1. Isaiah Berlin, *The Proper Study of Mankind*, Chatto and Windus, 1997, pp.239ff.
2. John Gray, *Berlin*, Fontana Press, 1995, p.71.
3. Berlin, *Concepts and Categories*, Hogarth Press, 1978, p.166.
4. Harris, *The Value of Life*, Routledge, 1994, p.10.
5. Ibid, p.18.
6. Ibid, p.19.
7. Ronald Dworkin, *Life's Dominion*, Harper Collins, 1993.
8. Ibid, p.32.
9. Ibid, p.33.
10. Ibid, p.184.

Chapter 6

1. Anthony Hirsh, 'Post-coital Sperm Revival', in *Human Reproduction*, vol.11, no.2, p.245.
2. Ibid.
3. M. Pembrey, 'A User's Guide', in T. Marteau and M. Richards (eds) *The Troubled Helix*, Cambridge University Press, 1996.
4. Jeremy Rifkin, *The Biotech Century*, Gollancz, 1998, p.12.
5. Ibid, p.14.

Selected Bibliography

Berlin, Isaiah (1977) *The Proper Study of Mankind*, Chatto & Windus.

BMA (1993) *Medical Ethics Today*, BMJ Publishing Group.

BMA (1998) *Human Genetics*, OUP.

Boswell, James (1981) *Christianity, Social Tolerance and Homosexuality*, Chicago University Press.

Countryman, L. William (1996) *Dirt, Greed and Sex*, SCM Press.

Dworkin, Ronald (1993) *Life's Dominion*, HarperCollins.

Dyson, Anthony (1994) *The Ethics of IVF*, Mowbray.

Engelhardt, H. Tristram (1991) *Bioethics and Secular Humanism*, SCM Press.

Foucault, Michel (1990, 1992) *The History of Sexuality* (3 vols), Penguin.

Harris, John (1992) *Wonderwoman and Superman*, OUP.

— (1994) *The Value of Life*, Routledge.

Jones, Steve (1994) *The Language of the Genes*, Flamingo.

Kelly, Kevin T. (1998) *New Directions in Sexual Ethics*, Geoffrey Chapman.

Leech, Kenneth (1998) *Drugs and Pastoral Care*, DLT.

MacIntyre, Alasdair (1982) *After Virtue*, Duckworth.

— (1997) *A Short History of Ethics*, Routledge.

Neitzsche, Friedrich (1990) *Beyond Good and Evil*, Penguin.

— (1996) *On the Genealogy of Morals*, OUP.

Rifkin, Jeremy (1998) *The Biotech Century*, Gollancz.

Claude Sureau and Françoise Shenfield (eds) (1995) *Ethical Aspects of Human Reproduction*, John Libbey Eurotext.

Tivnan, Edward (1996) *The Moral Imagination*, Simon & Schuster.

Tudge, Colin (1993) *The Engineer in the Garden*, Pimlico.

John Harris ?!.